W. H. Dixon

New America Vol. I.

Collection of British Authors

W. H. Dixon

New America Vol. I.
Collection of British Authors

ISBN/EAN: 9783742833495

Manufactured in Europe, USA, Canada, Australia, Japa

Cover: Foto ©Andreas Hilbeck / pixelio.de

Manufactured and distributed by brebook publishing software (www.brebook.com)

W. H. Dixon

New America Vol. I.

COLLECTION
OF
BRITISH AUTHORS.
VOL. 928.

NEW AMERICA BY W. H. DIXON.

IN TWO VOLUMES.

VOL. I.

NEW AMERICA.

BY

WILLIAM HEPWORTH DIXON,
AUTHOR OF "THE HOLY LAND," ETC.

COPYRIGHT EDITION.

IN TWO VOLUMES.
VOL. I.

LEIPZIG

BERNHARD TAUCHNITZ

1867.

The Right of Translation is reserved.

TO

CHARLES WENTWORTH DILKE, Esq.

OF

TRINITY HALL, CAMBRIDGE,

MY FELLOW-TRAVELLER IN THE GREAT WEST,

THESE VOLUMES

ARE AFFECTIONATELY INSCRIBED.

PREFACE.

SOME STUDIES of past times, which have long occupied my pen, led me last summer to the James River and to Plymouth Rock. I went out in search of an old world, and found a new one. East, west, north, and south, I met with new ideas, new purposes, new methods; in short, with a New America.

The men who planted these Free States — doing the noblest work that England has achieved in history — were spurred into their course by two great passions; a large love of Liberty; a deep sense of Religion; and, in our Great Plantation, liberty and religion exercise a power over the forms of social and domestic life unknown at home. In the heart of solid societies and conservative churches, we find the most singular doctrines, the most audacious experiments; and it is only after seeing what kind of forces are at work within them, that we can adequately admire the strength of these societies and churches.

What I saw of the changes now being wrought in the actual life of Man and Woman on the American soil, under the power of these master passions, is pictured in these pages.

6 ST. JAMES' TERRACE,
New Year's Day, 1867.

CONTENTS

OF VOLUME I.

		Page
CHAPTER I.	The Western Country	11
— II.	Bleeding Kansas	22
— III.	Overland Mail	32
— IV.	The Prairies	43
— V.	Prairie Indians	53
— VI.	The Red Man	60
— VII.	Indian Life	70
— VIII.	Carrying the Mail	81
— IX.	Red Communities	91
— X.	The Indian Question	98
— XI.	City of the Plains	107
— XII.	Prairie Justice	110
— XIII.	Sierra Madre	124
— XIV.	Bitter Creek	136
— XV.	Descent of the Mountains	147
— XVI.	The New Jerusalem	156
— XVII.	The Mormon Theatre	165
— XVIII.	The Temple	174
— XIX.	The Two Seers	182
— XX.	Flight from Bondage	190

CONTENTS OF VOLUME I.

			Page
CHAPTER XXI.	Settlement in Utah	. . . . .	196
— XXII.	Work and Faith	. . . . .	204
— XXIII.	Missionary Labour	. . . . .	210
— XXIV.	Mormon Light	. . . . .	217
— XXV.	Secular Notes	. . . . .	223
— XXVI.	High Politics	. . . . .	230
— XXVII.	Marriage in Utah	. . . . .	237
— XXVIII.	Polygamous Society	. . . . .	244
— XXIX.	The Doctrine of Pluralities	. . .	251
— XXX.	The Great Schism	. . . .	260
— XXXI.	Sealing	. . . . .	267
— XXXII.	Woman at Salt Lake	. . . .	275
— XXXIII.	The Republican Platform	. . .	286

NEW AMERICA.

CHAPTER I.

The Western Country.

"Guess these Yanks must look alive on this side the River, unless they should happen to enjoy having their eye-teeth drawn — eh, Judge?"

The man to whom this appeal is made as judge lifts up his chin from a dish of hominy and corned beef, glances first at myself, then at my fellow-traveller, and after winking an eye to the right and left, says slowly, "Guess you are right there, Sheriff."

Spoken, as it is, across the table of a tiny hotel in the city of Atchison — the only wonder about which hotel is, how a place so diminutive can hold so much dirt and feed so much vermin — this passage of legal wit may need a few words of explanation.

The Yanks now warned by the Sheriff that they must look alive, under penalty of having their eye-teeth drawn, are my friend Charles W. Dilke and myself; two men of undeniable English birth and blood. English faces are not seen every day in the

State of Kansas; and these Western boys (every man living beyond the Missouri is a Boy, just as every woman is a Lady — in her own right), these Western boys, having dim notions of ethnology and accent, set down every man who crosses the River with a white face and without a bowie-knife, as a Yankee — a traveller from the New England States in quest of gold-dust, reservations, and corner-lots. "The River" means the Missouri; here flowing between the settled State of that name and the wild unpeopled region, known in maps as Kansas, in poetry and fiction as Bleeding Kansas. To a Western boy, the Missouri is the Thames, the Rhine, and the Seine; his stream of commerce, beauty, luxury, and art; and every man and woman, that is to say, every boy and lady, living in the western uplands, beyond this margin of bluff and forest, talks to you about going down to the River just as a Picardic peasant boasts of going up to Paris, as a Marylebone grocer speaks of running down to Brighton and the Isle of Wight. The River divides him, as he says, from the East, from the States; and the current jest, everywhere to be heard from Atchison to Salt Lake, runs, that a man who means to cross the Missouri is going on a trip to America. Dressed in his high boots, his slouch hat, his belt, his buffalo-skin, his bowie-knife, and his six-shooter, a Western boy feels for the unarmed, sober, unadventurous men dwelling on the opposite bank of the River, the sort of proud contempt which an Arab beyond Jordan cherishes for the settlers in Galilee, spiced with the fierce hatred which a Spanish hidalgo dwelling east of the Duero, feels for the Portuguese pedlars crawling on the western bank.

Now, that question of drawing the eye-teeth is one about which I hold to an extreme opinion. Five or six years ago, when calling on my old friend Landor in his Florentine house, and expressing my joy at finding him so hale and bright (he was then eighty-four), I heard in reply to my congratulations, these noticeable words: "My dear fellow, say no more about it, I have lost four of my teeth." When I smiled, the veteran added, "Do not laugh at me; I would rather have lost all my intellect than one of my teeth." On the whole I should hardly go Landor's length, though the threat of having your "eye-teeth" drawn for you, willy nilly, is certainly one to disturb a saint. But we have crossed our Jordan, and on this side the River we must take our chance.

Early yesterday, a sultry August morning, we left St. Louis; a bright and busy city, full of a fierce and tameless life, half Saxon, half Latin; a city which has been smitten to the heart by panic, such as will sometimes fall upon Cairo and Aleppo in a time of plague. For a month of burning heat — the heat of a great plain, lying low down in the drain of a great continent three hundred miles from the nearest hills, eight hundred miles from a mountain range — cholera has been sweeping off her countless victims from those quays on which the poor Irish labour, from those slums in which the improvident negroes lodge.

No Howard Society sprang up this year to assist the poor as on a former visitation of the pest, when fifteen hundred of the young, rich, able men of the city had put their hearts into the helping work. Nothing had been done to meet a calamity which is always threatening such a city as St. Louis, built on one of the deepest sewers in the world. With a lack of wisdom hardly to be matched beyond the walls of Gotham, the council had ceased to make daily returns of the dead, the number of which could only be guessed from the march of funerals through the streets, and from the register of interments in the ten or twelve busiest graveyards. The rate of deaths ran high, and it was grossly extended by the arithmetic of fear. Fires were burning in every street; lime was being forced into every gutter; no one dared to enter a public conveyance; horrible tales,. the offspring of a Southern brain, were whispered in your ears at table, where you heard that every officer had flown from the cemeteries, even the felons and murderers who had been promised their pardon on condition of interring the victims of cholera; that the unburied corpses were heaped together in the island; that coffins and searcloths had been set on fire by the runaways; that a thousand nameless horrors had been committed in the dead-houses and in the graveyards. The deathbells were tolling day and night.

We left the city early. Noon saw us at Macon, picking grapes and sucking melons; midnight brought us to St. Joseph (affectionately called St. Joe), on the Missouri River, some dozen miles above Atchison, 'and of course on the eastern bank.

At two o'clock, in the night, we came to the end of our iron-track, when the car in which we rode emptied itself into a field, at no place in particular, but in a patch of waste land overgrown by Stink-weed, and in a situation generally supposed to be occupied by a ferry-boat.

When we came alongside the last plank of the railway, the night being bleak and chilly, it was sweet to hear the cry of the hotel-runner (a tout is here called a runner), "Any one for Planter's House?" Yes: we were all for Planter's House; and away we huddled, with our sacks and sticks, our wraps and overcoats, into an omnibus, which stood ready by the plank to swallow us up. Ugh! what monster is lying among our feet? Something like a huge black dog was sleeping on the floor; which, the moment we pushed into the doorway, began to snort and kick. It seemed too big for a dog: perhaps it was a bull, that finding the omnibus open, had crept in from the Missouri chills. Presently, it began to swear; such oaths as Uncle Toby heard in Flanders; and on waking into consciousness, the strange beast proved to be the driver, coiled up, concealed, and snoring in a buffalo's hide. Getting into our seats, with a dozen sleepless wretches like ourselves, we cried, "All right," and bade the driver "Go a-head."

"Guess you'll wait for the ferry," said he, with a volley of adjectives and objurgations, such as ladies and clergymen would consider high in flavour.

"When will the ferry-boat come over?" some one asked.

"Well, I guess about seven o'clock."

It was now two; the night raw and cold; the omnibus choked with passengers; and we were lying out in an open field. Shaking the hotel-runner from a doze — both he and the driver had again tumbled off into sleep, in the cosiest corner of our coach — we learned that the river might be crossed, at that point, even in the night, if we liked to venture upon it in a small rowing-boat. Venture upon it! Away we trudged, through the stink-weed, lugging our traps, which no one could be got to carry for us to the river side; feeling our feet down the bank, listening to the lap of the stream, and crying for help to the opposite bluffs. The bank was steep and soft, the black loam slipping beneath our shoes, while a dense yellow fog lay heavily on the swift and whirling flood. On the opposite heights we could trace the outlines of a little town; a few white houses scattered here and there; below which loomed the dark outline of the river bank. But where was the rowing-boat? Not on our side of the river; for Bill, the waterman, lodged in his wifeless cabin on the Kansas side; and a yep, yep — a war-whoop raised by the runner, which ought to have roused the seven sleepers from their trance — came back to us only in echoes from the Kansas bluffs. No boat came over with it; and after hanging by the waterside for an hour, seeing the fog grow thicker, and fancying the stream grow wider, we turned away from the muddy bank, not wholly displeased at our war-cry having failed to disturb the boatman's rest.

Going back to the omnibus, we found the driver

snorting in his nook. We shall never forget the volleys of oaths and growls which he fired off during the next four hours; neither shall we forget the rude and ready kindness with which he thrust upon us one of his blankets and his buffalo hide. My friend lay down and slept; sleep comes to you easily in youth; for myself, I walked on the plank; made a second trip to the river; watched the stars pale out; railed against the stink-weed; smoked a cigar.

At seven the ferry-boat came steaming over; at eight we are seated at table in the Planter's House, in the midst of these rough aristocrats of Kansas; a jolly set of dogs, each dog with a bowie-knife in his pocket, a six-shooter in his belt.

"Can you tell me, sir, at what hour the Overland Mail leaves Atchison for Salt Lake?" is the simple inquiry to which the Sheriff answers, as above, with that suggestion about our eye-teeth being hardly safe in Kansas. Not taking the reply so quickly as might be, I look the man steadily in the face, and repeat my question; this time with extreme deliberation; on which the company break into a pleasant burst of Satanic laughter. Then we hear from the judge that the Overland Mail (to travel by which, on our way to Denver and Salt Lake, we have come from St. Louis to Atchison, its starting-point) has ceased to run by the Platte route, and that the officers and stages have been sent down the river to Leavenworth, whence the mail is in future to be sent across the Plains by an easier and shorter line.

Mail, mail-agent, stock, mules, waggons, all have been sent down the river to Leavenworth, and we have no choice left us but to take up our traps and follow in their wake. These folks make merry at our expense, with a brutal kind of good nature; for a transfer of the Overland Mail from Atchison to Leavenworth is a big blow to their town, such as people who have put their money in it, and who are bound either to stand by it or fall with it, may be forgiven for not seeing in the light of a joke. Being regarded as companions in their misery, it is expected in the town that we shall consider ourselves generally as victims of a plot, and as having had one at least of our eye-teeth drawn.

In a hundred phrases we are told that the mail is leaving the best route through the Prairies for the worst. The Platte route, we hear, is safe and easy; a good road, well stocked and stationed; the military posts on which are strong, the Indians all through which are friendly to white men. In a word, it is the route. The new route is called the Smoky Hill route, from a rolling mist which runs along it for a hundred miles.

"Well, gentlemen," says the Sheriff, "you will see it, and then you will judge. Perhaps you like having your remaining eye-teeth drawn?"

One of these citizens takes from his pocket a gazette of the current date, in which there is news from the Smoky Hill country; showing that Black Kettle, Roman Nose, Spotted Dog, and some other worthies of the red race, are out on the war-path; telling how this and that lonely ranch has been plundered and fired by the Cheyennes; and giving lists of white men who have been killed by these savages. By the same gazette we learn that in the North the state of affairs is rather worse than better. A party of white men, coming down the Missouri, has been attacked by Blackfeet Indians, who exchanged shots with them, and swam after them, but were distanced by the rapidity with which the white men plied their boats. The party thus escaping from the tomahawk report that seven white men, coming in a boat down the same river, have been captured and killed by Crows, an Indian tribe who have recently made a treaty of peace with the government; but in consequence of some slight, as they allege, have burned their treaty, put on ochre and vermilion, and gone out, like their brethren the Cheyennes and Sioux, on the war-path.

A tall, swashing fellow, bickering with rifle, bowie-knife, and six-shooter, lounges into the room, and is introduced to us as Captain Walker; "the famous Captain Jem Walker, sir; who has crossed the Plains seven-and-twenty times; after whom Walker's Creek is named" — a creek of which we blush to think that we know nothing, not even the famous name. Captain Walker is of opinion that we shall be fools if we trust our scalps along the Smoky Hill route. The Platte road is the only safe one. When we object that as the mail no longer runs along that safer path, we can hardly travel by it, he opines that we shall do well to stay a few days in Atchison, during which he will put us up to the ropes, and fix us generally in Prairie politics. If we don't know what is best for ourselves, he has no objection to our being damned, as we certainly shall be after making unpleasant acquaintance with a Cheyenne knife.

It is clear that these men of Atchison have but a poor opinion of the Leavenworth route when compared against their own.

Hearing that a small steamer is going down the river to Leavenworth in the afternoon, we send for our bills, and have our boxes put on board. It is now nine in the morning, and as we have nothing to do, our new friends think proper to stay and help us; a courtesy on their side to which we should offer no objection if it were not for their frequent and sardonic allusions to the fact of our having been taken in. About noon an accident raises us in their good opinion to a height yet higher than that from which we had evidently fallen; enabling us to quit the town, morally speaking, sword in hand and with flying colours.

Sauntering down the street, enjoying our gossip and cigar, we note the word Post-office on a shop-front, and on going inside we find there is one letter with my name on the cover, written in an unknown hand, on which three cents are due. Paying the money, and breaking the seal, I find the letter is not for me; on which I fold and restore it to the postmaster, saying it is not mine, and should be kept for the owner, to whom it is perhaps of moment. Eyeing me in a queer way, the postmaster takes the letter, and gives me back my change, of three cents. "Do you see?" says the Sheriff to his nearest friend; "damned smart that — read his letter and got his money back! Hang me if I think they are Yanks after all."

One touch of roguery, it would seem, is enough to make the whole world kin!

CHAPTER II.

Bleeding Kansas.

"WELL, Sam," say I to a blithe young negro of thirty-five years, a boy with quick eye and delicate razor-hand, as he powders my face and dabs the rosewater on my hair, in the shaving-room of Planter's House, Leavenworth, "where were you raised?"

"Me riz in Missouri, sar."

"You were born a slave, then?"

"Yes, sar, me slave in Weston; very bad boss: always drunk and kicking poor nigger boy."

"And how did you get your freedom, Sam — did you go and fight?"

"No, sar; me no fight; tink fighting big sin; me swim."

"Swim! Oh, yes; you mean you swam across the Missouri into Kansas, from a slave state into a free state?"

"Dat true, sar. One bery dark night, me slip away from Weston; run through the wood along river bank, down stream; get into de water by dem trees, and push over to de mud bank" (pointing to the great ridge of slime which festers in front of Leavenworth when the water runs low); "there wait till morning, looking at the stars ob heaven and de lights in dese houses all about; and when daylight come, creep out of de rushes and wade ober to the levée."

"Then you were free?" Sam answers this question only by a grin.

"Had you any help in your escape from men on this side the river — the slaves had always good friends in Kansas?"

"No, sar; me got no help to 'scape; for me neber tell no one, 'cause me neber know afore the moment when me slip away. The Lord put it in my head. Me Methodist, sar; most nigger-boy in Missouri, Methodist; me just come home from chapel, tinking of de wonderful ways of de Lord, when some one say, close in my ear, 'Rise up, Sam; run away and be a man.' It was de voice of de Lord; I know it well. At first, I not see what to do; me tink it quite wrong to run away and steal myself from boss, — twelve hundred dollars. Den me tink, it must be right to obey de voice of de Lord, for me belong more to de Lord than to boss, and den I slip away into de woods."

"Of course, you were followed?"

"Yes, sar," says Sam, putting the last of his fine flourishes upon my face; "boss come ober into Leavenworth, where he find me in de street. 'Come here, you damned nigger,' he say, pulling out his revolver, and catching me by de neck. He got a boat all ready: den some people come up, 'You let dat nigger go alone,' say one; 'Put a knife into de damned nigger,' say another. Den come a big row; dey fight for me all day; and my side win."

The date of this little history was six short years

ago. Missouri, the fertile state beyond the river, the forests of which I have before me as I write, was then a slave state, with a sparse but fiery population of slave-breeders and slave-dealers. Nine years before that time — that is to say, so late as 1851, when the world was gathering for its jubilee of progress in Hyde Park — all this wide region, lying westward of the Missouri, from this river bank to the Rocky Mountains, was without a name. A host of wild Indian tribes, Kansas, Cheyennes, Arappahoes, hunted over the great Plains; following the elk, the buffalo, the antelope, to their secret haunts. Two great lines of travel had been cut through the Prairies; one leading southward to Santa Fé in New Mexico, the other running westward, by the Platte river, towards Salt Lake and San Francisco; but the country was still an Indian hunting-ground, in which the white man could not lawfully reside. Half-a-dozen forts had been thrown up by the Government in this Indian country — Fort Bent, Fort Laramie, Fort Leavenworth, Fort Calhoun, Old Fort — but rather with a view to guarding the red man's rights than to helping the white traveller and trader in their need. But while the people of all nations were assembling in Hyde Park, and wondering at the magnificent country which had even then to be represented by an empty space, a swarm of settlers crossed the Missouri on rafts and in canoes, seized upon the bluffs between Fort Calhoun and Fort Leavenworth, threw up camps of log-huts, staked out the finest patches of land, especially those on the banks of creeks and pools, and so laid the foundation of what are now the populous and flourishing towns of Omaha, Nebraska, Atchison, and Leavenworth — cities of the free Territory of Nebraska, of the free State of Kansas.

Then commenced along the whole line of the Missouri river, that fitful, sanguinary strife, which earned for this region the mourning epithet of Bleeding Kansas. It lasted six years, and was a prelude to the civil war.

Lawrence and Leavenworth were the results of this battle, of which Sam's little story may be taken as a sample.

Every one is aware that in the great feud between the free-soilers and the slave-holders of America, a truce had been made in 1820, which is known in history as the Missouri Compromise; by which act it was arranged between the parties that slavery should never be introduced into any western region lying beyond 36° 30' of north latitude, excepting into such portion of Missouri as happened to stand above that line. For thirty years that truce held good, and even when the war of freedom raged against slavery on other fields, the Missouri Compromise was respected in the west. As the final conflict neared, the two parties in the struggle showed an equal discontent with that act of truce. The slave-owners in Missouri, having an exceptional advantage in their state of settling with their slaves above the prohibited line, desired to carry their domestic institution straight backward through the country in their rear to the foot of the Rocky Mountains, even if they should not be able to carry it thence to the Pacific Ocean. All the South went with them in their plans; though their action was in open conflict with the law. Secret societies sprang up in many states — Blue Lodges, Social Bands, Sons of the South, and many more — all pledged to aid these planters in carrying slavery westward of the Missouri river, in the teeth of their own Compromise, in violation of their own truce.

The slave-holders of Missouri won one victory without a shot; in quietly, by a local act, which attracted no attention either in Boston or in New York, extending their own frontier westward, from the line drawn north and south through Kansas City, up to that of the river bank; adding six large and now populous counties to their state, and consequently to the area of the slave empire. This act was absolutely illegal; but no one in the eastern cities noted it until the bills effecting the change had become law, and the district had been peopled with masters and their slaves. The game appeared to be wholly in their hands. From this new slave soil, which lies on the opposite bank, in front of my window, Blue Lodges, Social Bands, and Sons of the South streamed over into these Delaware reserves, into these Kansas hunting-grounds; each boss, accompanied by his sons and his negroes, proceeding to help himself to the choicest lots. From St. Louis to New Orleans their courage was applauded, their success predicted. In Washington the slave-dealing senators, instead of calling these Missourian planters to account, and carrying out the law against them, sustained them in this outrage on the free states.

By a course of partisan agitations they procured a fresh compromise, in which it was agreed that the question of slavery should be referred back, generally, to the people of any unorganised country claiming to come within the Union either as a Territory or as a State. Such an act was supposed by the planters of Missouri and Kentucky to be an open declaration that Kansas and Nebraska were to be organised as slave territories. But now New England came into the field. The conversion of Nebraska from free soil into slave soil would have carried the line of slavery, in the western country, as high north as Boston! A Northern Emigrant Aid Society was founded in Massachusetts, sturdy farmers, fervent professors, youthful poets, yoked horses to their waggons, and pushed across the continent towards the Missouri, sworn to settle on the new Indian lands, to accept the compromise of Congress, and, in their quality of free citizens, to vote a free constitution for Kansas. The Blue Lodges were already hutted at Leavenworth and Atchison, and when the first New Englander crossed the stream, being unable to answer these sentinels that he owned any niggers, they placed him in an open boat, without food, without oars, and sent him floating down the river amidst derisive shouts and threats. A meeting of Sons of the South was called in Westport, on the Kansas border, but within the limits of Missouri, at which, after fiery eloquence, the following resolution was unanimously carried:

"That this association will, whenever called upon, by any of the citizens of Kansas Territory, hold itself in readiness together to assist and remove any and all immigrants who go there under the auspices of the Northern Emigrant Aid Society."

The "Squatter Sovereign," a news sheet, published in the town of Atchison (founded and named by David Atchison, Senator of Missouri), put forth in an early number this declaration of the planters:

"We will continue to lynch and hang, tar and feather, and drown, any white-livered abolitionist who dares to pollute our soil."

In July, 1854, thirty New England free-soilers crossed the river in open boats; they were well armed, and brought with them tents and provisions. Pushing up the Kansas river, they rested at the foot of a fine bluff, in the midst of a rolling prairie, covered with flowers. Pitching their tents, and beginning to fell wood for shanties, they called the place at which they camped the city of Lawrence, from the name of their popular purse-holder. In August they were joined by seventy more: men like themselves, well armed and resolute, prepared to found that city, and to free that soil. Now had arrived the time for the Missouri men to show their spirit; a hundred Yankees, separated from their friends by six great States, had come into their midst; daring them to carry out their threat of either hanging, lynching, or drowning every one who should cross into Kansas without a negro slave in his train. Three hundred and fifty Sons of the South took horse, dashed over the shallow stream, and, having early in the morning formed a camp and thrown out piquets, sent word into Lawrence that these new settlers must quit the Territory, promising never to return. Three hours were given the free-soilers in which to pack their things and get ready to march. A Yankee bugle summoned the immigrants to arms; a civil but decisive answer was returned to the Missouri camp; and when the Sons of the South perceived that the Yankees were ready for the fray, and would be likely to fight it out so long as a man could hold his piece, they began to suspect each other, to doubt the goodness of their carbines, and to steal away. Dusk found their camp much thinned, dawn found it broken up and gone.

From that day Lawrence has grown and prospered. More than once it has fallen into Missourian hands, and the marks of grape and canister are seen upon some of its buildings; but its free-soil people have never been driven out, and it is now a charming little city, with the brightness of a New England town. It is the capital of a free State.

In these streets of Leavenworth many a fierce battle has been fought; the Sons of the South living close at hand, in a score of villages on yon wooded banks. Blood has been shed in almost every lane, especially at the voting times, when thousands of the Missourians used to come across in boats, take possession of the polling-booths, and return an overwhelming but fictitious majority in favour of a slave constitution. One good citizen, William Phillips, an advocate, was seized by Sons of the South for having signed a protest, as a lawyer, against the frauds which had disgraced the election; was forced into a boat, and pulled up the river to Weston, on the Missouri side; where he was first tarred and feathered, then ridden on a rail, afterwards put up to auction as a slave, and finally knocked down, amidst frantic yells and menaces, to a negro. On his escape from Weston, Phillips returned to Leavenworth, resolute in his free-soil faith, and ready for the post of danger in every fray.

In another week from this date, it will be just ten years since a gang of Blue Lodges started from the opposite bank, landed on this levée, took possession of the town, which lay completely at their mercy for many hours, and under pretence of searching for arms — an utterly illegal search on their part — plundered and insulted the free-soilers in every house. Phillips refused to allow these fellows to come inside his door; on which the house was attacked and its owner killed. Before he fell, Phillips had shot two of his assailants dead. His house was burned to the ground, along with many other dwellings; and every free-soiler who could be found in Leavenworth was put on board a steamer and sent down the river.

Yet the New Englanders rallied to their flag, with growing numbers and glowing passions; becoming genuine settlers on the land, which the Missouri men were not. Here, and elsewhere, it has been shown that slavery, as a social system, lacked the solid fibre of a colonising power. Slaves could not work the prairie land to profit; negroes, toiling under a master's eye and whip, require the rich soils of Mississippi and Alabama. With a pistol in one hand, a hoe in the other, these stout New Hampshire and Massachusetts lads fought on, toiled on, not only until they had gained a fair majority in the ballot-boxes, but won a full ascendancy in the open field.

One of the comic incidents of this war was the Battle of Black Jack, when Captain Clay Pate, (ominous name!) a Virginian, who gave himself airs as a professional soldier, put himself at the head of fifty-six Sons of the South, and threatened to eat up old John Brown, of Osawatomie (afterwards, unhappily, of Harper's Ferry) and his band of twenty-seven free-soilers. Pate had organised his force like a little army, with its horse and foot, its camp equipage, and its luggage train; and having just then been plundering Palmyra, a free-soil city, his baggage mules were heavily laden with the spoils of war. Brown made a fair fight, by going out into the open plains. After a lusty tug, Clay Pate surrendered to the tough old fellow — himself, with his sword, his luggage train, all the spoils of Palmyra, twenty-one hale men, the whole of his dead and wounded, and his gorgeous tent.

In 1861, a few months after these citizens of Leavenworth had fought the battle for my friend Sam on this levée under my windows, the wounds of Bleeding Kansas were staunched and healed by her admission into the Union as a free state.

CHAPTER III.

Overland Mail.

The Overland Mail is one of the many great facts of the Great Republic. The postal returns tell you how many, you can imagine how important, are the letters going westward from the Atlantic cities to the Pacific cities. This mail is an Imperial institution.

While we were yet in London, dreaming of the details of our trip to the Rocky Mountains, it was always comforting to know that in going out among the wild Cheyennes and Sioux, we should find ourselves travelling in company with the Imperial Mail. Glancing at maps, scanning the vast spaces over which Cheyenne, Sioux, Comanche and Arappahoe roam, one is apt to think there may lurk some spice of danger in such a journey; but then comes in the assuring thought that all along this route across the Prairies, across the Mountains, the American mails are being daily sent under powerful escorts of mounted men. Magic lies in this word "daily." That which is daily done must be safely done. Would he not be considered a sorry fellow who should fear to travel, even along a road infested by Sioux and rattlesnakes, under escort of United States troops in company with the Imperial Mail? When Speaker Colfax drove across the Plains last fall, to study the

Indian question, the Mining question, and the Mormon question, among living Indians, Miners, and Mormons, instead of reading about them in government reports, he had only one general officer, one colonel, and twenty-four sabres galloping round his coach; yet he has publicly confessed that — although the red-skins frightened him a little, and delayed his journey much, by plundering the stations in his front, and threatening every moment to have his scalp — he got safely through to Denver and Salt Lake.

Colfax, it is true, was a state official, and besides having his escort, he had also with him a considerable party of well-armed men. We are strangers, only two in number (so far as we can see); we are but slightly armed with Colts — since we have all along been dreaming, that if any fighting is to be done, it will be the work of our gallant escort, riding by our sides in defence of the Imperial Mail.

At Leavenworth we find the mail-agents, to whom we have letters from their chief in New York — as we have to every one employed by the Overland Mail Company along these tracks. Nothing can be more polite, more teasing, than their answers to our questions. Everything shall be done for us that can be, under the circumstances. We have come at an unlucky time. If we had only started a month sooner — if we had only stayed a month later — all would have been right. As it is, they will do their best; we may find things a little rough in the Plains, but the agents have hardly any doubt that we shall get through to our journey's end.

Such words rather pique our fancies; since our health, our comfort, nay our lives, depend on the state of these Plains. The fact is, the old road by way of the Platte River has been changed, by order of Congress, for a shorter cut through the vast Indian region of the Smoky Hill Fork; a shorter course, perhaps a better one, if the road had only first been made, bridged, and levelled; and if the Indian tribes who hunt buffalo and antelope across it had been either driven away or negotiated into peace. None of these things have yet been done.

Two great lines of travel have been driven by the white men through these Plains: (1) the Platte road from Omaha and Atchison, by way of Kearney, Denver, and Salt Lake City, to San Francisco; (2) the Arkansas route, starting from Kansas City, and running by Fort Atkinson and Fort Wise to Puebla, the gold regions of Colorado, and thence to San Francisco. To the existence of these two roads the Indians seem to have submitted in despair. To the Platte road, they have ceased to show any strong opposition; having fought for it and lost it; first to the Mormon pilgrims, afterwards to the gold-seekers, men who came into their country, driving before them trains of waggons, in bands of eighty or a hundred, and being armed with rifles and revolvers. To the Arkansas road they nurse a sharper antipathy; since it is mainly a trial road, the right to travel over which has been purchased from their chiefs. Still, though it may be with a bad grace, and with many murmurs and protests, they have shown, and they still show, themselves ready to respect the white man as he passes through their lands by either of these two routes. But in the vast prairies between these tracks lie the great buffalo-runs, with the pastures feeding nearly all that remains in the Indian Territories of the elk, the antelope, and the black-tailed deer. The buffalo-runs are also theirs, say the Cheyennes and the Arappahoes, and they must either keep them free from whites or else die like dogs. They say they will not die before the pale-faces; therefore, they must keep the buffalo-runs of Kansas and Colorado (as the white men have begun to call the plains — on paper) free from intrusion of mail and train.

Now the new route chosen by Congress for the Overland Mail, beyond all question a shorter line from St. Louis to San Francisco, cuts these buffalo-runs, these elk and antelope pastures, into two halves, and, as the Cheyennes and their allies, the Comanches, Arappahoes, Kiowas, Sioux and Appaches, know very well, a railway is being built in the rear of this new mail; a railway which has already reached Wamego, near Fort Riley. Now the red men, knowing that the Mail is only a herald of much worse, and that the railway bell will quickly follow the crack of a driver's whip, have called a council of their tribes, and some say have concluded to try a war against the whites for the possession of these buffalo-runs. When a railway engine, say the braves, shall have whistled away buffalo and antelope, it will be idle to raise the hatchet and draw the bow. Now is the time for them to strike; now or never; and, even if a few of the old men, grey with years and sad with sorrow, should recommend peace with their white neighbours, resignation to the will of their Great Spirit, the young braves, proud of their own strength, ignorant of the white men's numbers and resources, are said to be all for war. If the pale-face will not come into the buffalo-runs, they will keep the peace; if he will build his ranch, dig his well, and crop his grass, in these runs, the Cheyennes and the Arappahoes, aided by their brethren of the Prairie and the hill country, will burn his shanty and take his scalp.

Such are the rumours that we hear from every mouth in Kansas. A small party, it is true, affects to regard the alarm of Leavenworth, Lawrence, and Wamego, as a panic having little or no foundation; partisans of the new route by way of Smoky Hill Fork, who wish to see it opened and kept open. They are few in number; and I do not hear that any of these heroes propose to settle, as yet, along the line of road through the Cheyenne country.

Now, as we gather from the mail-agents in Leavenworth, this is the line along which we are to go a journey of thirteen hundred miles; through a country, the greater part of which has never been surveyed, through which there is no road, in which there are many streams and gullies, but not a single bridge; a country in which the hills, the creeks, the rivers, have as yet received no names, and in which the small military posts of the United States, themselves only corrals of logs and planks, lie two hundred miles apart.

Still, a line along which a mail so magnificent as that sent off from New York to San Francisco, not to speak of the thousand inferior cities which help to feed it, has been running its daily course, must be at least as safe as the line from Damascus to Banias. But on our saying this, or something like this, to a friend in Leavenworth, we learn, to our surprise, that there has never been a daily mail running along that line; that no such thing has ever yet been attempted; that there are neither men nor mules along the road to carry a daily mail; that, in point of fact, only one waggon, an empty waggon, has gone out in advance of us; that no one knows where that empty waggon is, or whether it will arrive in safety beyond the Plains.

We look at our pistols, and feel the hair on our polls; the aspect of affairs is at once tragic and comic; and the kindly jokes of our friends in Pall Mall, as to the best way of enjoying a scalping-knife, are coming rather near and hot. We find, too, that we are the only passengers booked for the trip; so that the number of revolvers coming into play, in case of a scrimmage with the Cheyennes and Comanches, in aid of the military escort, seems to be reduced to two. All our acquaintance in this city urge us to get more and better arms; a suggestion in which the mail-agents cordially agree. The new arm of the west, called a Smith-and-Wesson, is a pretty tool; as neat a machine for throwing slugs into a man's flesh as an artist in murder could desire to see. Bowie-knives, and suchlike, being useless to a Britisher who may have seen, but never practised, the art of ripping up an adversary's side, like a Livornese and a Valentian, we buy a couple of these Smith-and-Wessons, and then pay our fare of five hundred dollars to Salt Lake. An escort of veterans from the Potomac, aided by these six-shooters, will surely scare away all the Cheyennes, Arappahoes, and Sioux, who may be found clamouring about the rights of man, especially about the rights of red men, in the buffalo-runs.

The rail has been laid down so far west as Wamego — the Clear Springs — so called from the fact of there being no water in the village; and there we are to join the stage for our long ride; the stage being an old and much-worn Concord coach; a vehicle of a kind unknown in Europe, though its shapelessness and inconvenience might be hinted by cutting off the coupé of a French diligence, and bellying out the rotundo, until it could be supposed by its proprietor big enough to hold nine persons. This coach, when we come to it, is jammed full of mail-bags — forty-two hundredweight in all — state despatches, love-letters, orders, bills of exchange, invoices of account, all sorts of lively and deadly missiles, the value of which to governor, maid, clerk, banker, emigrant, and dealer, must be far beyond price; and here are five passengers on the books to take their chances of the road (three of them being a young woman and two babies), who, having duly paid their fares and got their tickets, have a right to be taken on. But this going on is a thing impossible; as a glance at the coach and the mail-bags tells the experienced eye of the Wamego agent. What shall be done? The mail must go, even though the passengers should have to wait in Wamego for a month; and as the driver is already cracking his whip, and belching out volleys of oaths, which the lady and her two babies are obliged to hear (poor things!), the agent quickly makes up his mind, bids us get aboard — men and revolvers — says one sharp word to the driver, when away we plunge into the dust, leaving our female fellow-traveller, astonished, protesting, in the cloud of mud and sand. We look at each other wonderingly; for in this Paradise of Women, a petticoat is accustomed to carry all things before it — — the best room at an hotel, the highest place at table, the first seat in a coach, in spite of your prior right. Ha! the revolvers have done it. As we are dashing off, we look out of window for the troops who are to be our companions in the Cheyenne country. None are in sight! "The escort," says the agent, "will join you at Junction City, if there should seem to be any need; you must consider the mail as starting from Junction City;" and as he courteously waves his hand, we roll away into the dust.

In a couple of hours we pass Fort Riley; in two or three more we are at Junction City; a city of six wooden shanties, where we alight to sup off hot cake, tea, and tomatoes; and about an hour later, in the midst of a pleasant chat with the landlord of our hostelry, we hear the driver's cry, "On board!" Rushing out into the night, our belts swung round us, our pistols loaded for the fray, we find that our big Concord coach has been exchanged for a light prairie waggon, smaller in size, frailer in build, without a door, with very bad springs, and with canvas blinds for windows. Into this waggon, the letter-bags have been forced by an ingenious violence, the art of which is only known in the western country, with so neat a finish that it would seem impossible to insert two human beings between the mail-bags and the wall. But, in time, by doubling our legs across each other, by craning our necks, by slinging our elbows into straps, the feat is accomplished; the two human beings afore-named having been persuaded, much against the grain, to wriggle themselves between the bags, under a promise that the said bags will shake down in a few minutes so as to give plenty of room. This is not easy, we suggest to each other, since we have our own small litter of pistols, books, maps, brandy-flasks, shawls, night-caps, potted meats, cigar-cases, sticks, umbrellas, and the like, about our feet. We begin to fear, that unless the load shall happen to shake down considerably, we may chance to have a bad week of it.

But see, this fellow is about to start, though the escort is not in sight!

Whew! We speak to the agent: "Well," says he, in effect, "the officer in charge will not lend us any troops; his command is very low just now; the country is disturbed by Indians in his front and flank; he has enough to do to hold his own in the post. But," the good-natured agent adds, for our comfort, "you will find the road all right; some troops went up the Plains yesterday; you will pass them a-head; good-bye!" And we are off.

The truth now flashes on our minds like a revelation:

We are the escort!

Not a soul goes out with the mail, either now or through the journey, except the boy who drives the mules (changed every forty or fifty miles on the road); no escort, no mail agent, nobody save ourselves. I cannot say that in my travels, I have ever seen the fellow of this prairie mail. In the most dangerous district crossed by traveller and trader west of Chinese Tartary, the New York and St. Louis people trust the most important mail leaving any city in the world, excepting that from London, without a guard. No one doubts that the Cheyennes and Sioux are now holding council on these Plains, even if they have not as yet gone out upon the war-path; nay, that they have given notice, after their Indian manner, of an intention to stop the road; yet, the mail is going into their buffalo-runs, in spite of all warnings, without a single guard, even such an old fogie as used to blow his horn and shoulder his blunderbuss on Hounslow Heath.

Perhaps I am forgetting the confidence which they place in their English guard. They know that we are armed; they feel a reasonable certainty that we know how to use our tools. "The road is a little rough," says one of the stock-keepers as we roll from his station into the black midnight and the unknown prairie; "but the government will do nothing for us, until it has been roused by a great disaster; they care nothing for a few lives, especially for the lives of poor teamsters and drivers." One passing friend rather hopes that we may be scalped, as he thinks that such an event might create a pleasant and profitable sensation in New York.

We have paid five hundred dollars for escorting the United States mail to Salt Lake. It is a high price, but the privilege might be worth the cost, if we had a mind to use the facilities which fall about our feet and court us to see them. This mail is wholly at our mercy. Six nights and days we are shut up with our pistols and the United States correspondence; our sole companion being the boy outside, who cannot see into the waggon when the flaps are down. In one place a bag falls out of the waggon, and would certainly be left behind on the plain, but that we call the driver to stop and pick it up. In another place one of the bags bursts open, when a stream of letters comes flowing about our feet. We have only to help ourselves; read what we like, pocket what we like. Might not the secrets of a single letter be worth, in some hands, more than the five hundred dollars we have paid to guard them?

CHAPTER IV.

The Prairies.

Of all the States and Territories which still exist on paper, Kansas may be described as the Prairie State. Nebraska, Colorado, and the Indian territory, are covered by prairies; great grassy plains, not level, as many persons think, but rolling uplands, rising from the river to the mountains in a series of ascending billows, always of gentle grade, often of enormous sweep. But Kansas is beyond dispute the region in which these plains display themselves on the largest scale, and with their points most perfect.

On the old maps, which show the natural history of each section of the Great Republic, the district now called Kansas will be found figured by a buffalo, as Nebraska is marked by an antelope, Iowa by a beaver, Utah by a bear. Across these Plains, up from the Indian territory on the south, come the wild and multitudinous herds on which the Cheyennes, the Arappahoes, the Comanches, and the Kiowas feed.

For two hundred miles westward from the Missouri, the plains are green with trees, most of all so along the lines of the Kansas river and its many creeks and inlets. The wood is hickory, walnut, oak, and water-elm. Maple and chestnut are not found in the plains. The land is alive with shrubs and flowers; among which flourish wild marigolds, shamrock, water-lily (in the pools), rosin-weed, stink-weed, and sun-flowers. These sun-flowers of the West are not the tawny gauds of our cottage gardens; big and brazen bachelors, flourishing on a single stalk; but little golden flowers, clustering in bunches, and, like our buttercups, numberless as the stars of heaven. In many parts, the prairie is alive with their golden light. A white frame house — on this side of the river called a ranch — peeps out here and there from beneath the foliage, having its green blinds, its bit of garden, its sheep-fold. Herds of horses can be seen on the rolling plateau. Here you have a drove of cattle, there a long waggon train. Anon we pass an Indian village, where some families of Delawares, sent out from those Atlantic forests now occupied by the quays and palaces of Dover, Baltimore, and Philadelphia, have taken a fitful and precarious root in the soil. These Delawares have long since buried the hatchet, put on pantaloons, forgotten the use of war-paint. Some of them make farmers; living on friendly terms with their pale neighbours; even marrying their sons into the families of whites. We pass a Shawnee village, of which the same things may be said. White men's ranches stand among them; dangerous neighbours to these natives; for the Pale-face, finding his way through the cracks and crannies of Indian character, making himself first useful, then formidable, to the tribe, commonly ends the connexion with them by becoming lord and owner of their lands.

The air is warm and sweet; a perfume of prairie flowers mingling with the distant snows of the sierras. The sky is intensely blue, with none of that golden haze which frets the eye in our own southern landscapes. A patch of cloud, intense and vivid in its whiteness, dots and relieves the grand monotony of azure, so as to combine in one field of view the distinctive beauties of a Sicilian and an English sky.

As we draw away from the river, the woodland scenery disappears; the country opens to the right and left; the plains swell languidly into greater breadths of upland. About the creeks and pools, for the most part dry on the surface, there are still some shrubs; the wild convolvulus is common; also the Virginian creeper; more than all others a plant called the rosin-weed. This rosin-weed appears to be Nature's choice in the way of verdure and adornment. When the ground is either cleared by fire, or cut by the prairie breaker, the rosin-weed disappears; the fire-weed springs up in its place, and dies in its turn after two or three crops, in some places after one crop; when this second weed is succeeded by the tickle-grass. (P. S. Don't let the tickle-grass get up your legs — for it seems to be alive; to know you don't like it, and to creep up your pantaloons the faster you fret and worry.) After this grass come three or four species of wild grasses; and after these fertilizers sown by nature have dropped their decaying blades into the ground, the farmer may come with his rake and his seed to a soil made ready for his use.

Driving on night and day (as men must drive who have charge of an imperial mail), we begin to leave all trace of man and his arts, save one, behind. A prairie hen clucks in the wild sage; a rattlesnake coils among the sun-flowers; a wolf steals noiselessly along the road; dead mules, dead horses, dead oxen, strew the path, on which the carrion crow, the raven, and the wolf, find food; these white horns and skeletons of man's servants being often the only traces of his ever having found his way across the Plains.

By daring, ingenuity and patience, the Western trader has pushed a way for himself across this difficult tract of land; making an opening for trade and travel between the Atlantic and Pacific Oceans. He has done this feat as a private man, without help from the State, without cheers from any learned body, at a cost of blood and money which can never be counted upon earth; and for this reason: the Western man thinks nothing of blood, not much of treasure, when he regards them as being invested in a business that will pay. Holding his life in his hand, this reckless, jovial fellow, swearing overmuch, brimming with help when help is of use, is careless of blood, — either his own or yours, — far beyond an Arab, almost beyond a Chinese. This path through the prairie has been paved by him, again and again, with bones: but the trace of his passage, of his suffering, dies away out of sight with the autumnal flowers. Nature is here too strong for man to do more than throw a trail upon her landscape, which may show itself for a day in the bunch-grass, among the grey sand, and then vanish from sight like the track of a ship at sea. The prairie is not man's home. Even if he had time to plant and reap it, he could hardly grow a blade of grass, a stalk of Indian corn, on these open flats, where myriads of locusts clatter through the air, devouring in their hunger every green leaf and twig. We ride past a lonely ranch, near which the daring and hopeful tenant had planted a field with corn, for his winter food. Look at the poor man's harvest! Legions of locusts are upon his crop; and every ear that should have made him bread has been picked away.

In these uplands, Nature is lord and king. Snipes and plovers abound; blackbirds, carrion crows, ravens, and vultures are also seen. Flowers are still common; most of all, the dwarf sun-flower, which is sown so thickly through the landscape as to give it a shimmer of burning gold. The dwarf sun-flower is, in fact, *the* prairie flower; lighting up the face of Nature everywhere in our route, from the Missouri river to the Great Salt Lake; in some parts growing low and stunted, the stalk not a foot long, the flower not higher than a common marigold, in others rising ten or twelve feet high, with clusters of flowers, each flower as big as a peony. Ants are toiling in the ground; the little prairie dogs — comedians of the waste — sit crowing on their mounds of earth, until we drive close up to them, when they utter a quick laugh, and with a shout of mockery, plunge into their holes, head downwards, disappearing from our sight with a last merry wag of their tails. Owls, prairie-dogs, and rattle-snakes, live on the most friendly terms with each other; the owls and snakes dwelling in the prairie-dogs' holes, and sometimes, I fancy, eating the dogs when they happen to be short of food. It may only be a superstition; but the teamsters and drivers across the Plains have a fixed belief that flesh of the prairie-dog is poisonous in a peculiar way, and that men who eat of it become insane. Once, in a stress of hunger, I was obliged to kill one.

."Lord!" cries the boy at the ranch, "you will never eat that, sir."

"Why not? I am hungry enough to eat a Cheyenne."

"Well, sir," says the lad, "we prairie folks consider the owl, the rattle-snake, and the prairie-dog to be all of a kith and kin, the Devil's own spawn, and that anybody who eats them will go mad."

"Put him in the pan; I must take my chance." The flesh proved to be delicious, with something like the taste of squirrel; and on seeing me suck the savoury bone, the prairie-boy instantly seized and devoured a leg. I hope the teamsters and drivers will continue in their want of faith as to the wholesomeness of prairie-dogs; for the antics of these little animals should make them dear to every man who has to cross these Plains, in which the supply of comedy is extremely scant.

After passing Fort Ellsworth — a collection of wooden shanties, in which lie a hundred men, not very well armed (we hear), and careful to keep their feet within bounds, leaving the Cheyennes and Arappahoes alone — we have before us a stretch of two hundred and twenty miles of dangerous country, without a single post for its protection; a country in which there is no town, no camp, no ranch, except the log-stables, now being built for the overland mules. We are alone with Nature and the imperial mail. Around us, we have many signs that the Cheyennes and Arappahoes are hovering nigh; at times we catch visible evidence of a scout on some distant ridge of the Smoky Hill, and see the curl of blue smoke from some neighbouring creek.

We are now, between Big Creek and Big Timber station, in the very heart of the wild game country; a country of long, low, rolling hills, covered with a short sweet grass — bunch-grass — on which the buffalo loves to feed. We have ceased firing at rattlesnakes and prairie chickens; reserving our cartridges for the nobler uses of self-defence; though we are tempted, now and then, to try a shot at some elk, or antelope, or black-tailed deer. The great game being buffaloes, against the tough hides of which our small six-shooters are of no avail, we sit quietly in our waggon watching the herds troop by; in lines, in companies, in droves, in armies, the black and shaggy beasts go thundering in our front; sometimes from north to south, sometimes from south to north; but always scudding in our front, and always across our line of march. The plains are teeming with life; most of all with buffalo bulls and cows. For forty hours we have now had them always in our sight; thousands on thousands, tens of thousands after tens of thousands; a countless host of untamed animals; all of them fit for human food; enough, we should think, to stock Arappahoe, Comanche, and Cheyenne wigwams to the end of time. Once or twice the driver tries a shot; but fear of the red-skins commonly checks his wish to fire.

This buffalo, which is the white man's sport, is also the red man's food; and a Cheyenne warrior cannot be made to see why a Pale-face should come into his country and destroy the buffalo for the sake of a little amusement. A white man who has to kill buffalo to live, the Indian can comprehend, though he may have to suffer in estate by that white man's rifle; but a man who shoots buffalo for sport, having no wish to eat it, is a mystery to which any red-skin would gladly put an end by tomahawk and scalping-knife.

As we ascend the Plains, a series of rolling steppes, in no part level for a dozen miles, the sun grows fiercer overhead, the sands hotter beneath our feet. Snakes, lizards, locusts, swarm on the ground and in the air; the heat is terrible; sometimes, in the breathless noon, reminding me of the Jordan valley. Water is scarce and bad, and the dry, hot fever of external nature creeps into and corrupts your blood.

The fourth day of our journey on the plains is one of tropical warmth. That short, sweet grass on which the buffalo loves to feed, is now behind us in the lower plains, where moisture, though it may be scant, is not unknown, as it seems to be here for many a league on league. Our path is strewn with skeletons of oxen, mules, and horses; waste of the life that helps to keep up an overland trade from the river to the sea. Ravens and wolves are seen fattening on these remains of mule and ox; tame enough to be hardly scared from their meal by the crashing of our waggon-wheels through the burning sand. A golden haze, the effect of heat, envelopes the earth, and the mirage tantalizes our parching throats with a promise of water, — never to be reached. A stillness as of death is round about us. In the west we see a little cloud, not bigger, when we see it first, than a prairie-dog; anon it is the size of a fox, of a buffalo, of a mountain; in a few minutes it has covered the sky with one black and sulphurous pall, out of which the lightnings begin to leap and dance.

A flash comes through the still and silent air, like a gun-shot, suddenly, with a sharp surprise. It is followed by a wail of wind and rain, which lifts the sand from the ground into the air, and drives it into the canvas flaps of our mountain waggon, splashing us with mud and mire. No care can keep the deluge out; and in a few minutes we are drenched and smothered. Four or five hours that storm of sand and rain drives heavily against us. Two or three times the mules stand still in fear; turn their backs to the heavenly fire, refusing to go forward under any encouragement of either voice or whip. Were they not fastened to the coach, they would fly before the tempest; bolting for their lives until the hurricane should have drooped and died. Being chained to the waggon, they can only stand and moan. When the storm is spent, the stars come peeping out; the air is chill and sweet; and we drag our way along the wet and smoking plain.

Want of sleep, want of food, want of exercise — for we are jolted over the unmade tracks all night, all day, stopping at the creeks for a little water, at the log-stables for a change of mules, but a few moments only — have made us ill. We obtain no proper supplies of food and drink, and we are cooped up in a waggon designed (one might suppose) by some infernal genius as a place of torture; a machine in which you can neither sit, nor stand, nor lie down. My friend is suffering from bilious sickness; I am tormented by eruptions on the skin; yet, even with these quick monitors of evil in us, we are every day astonished by the sudden gush of life, which comes with the morning light. We crawl from our miserable den — a den without a door, without a window, without a step — with nothing save a coarse canvas cover for a roof, coarse canvas flaps for sides, — into the dust and filth of a stable; banged and beaten and jolted, until our heads are swollen, our faces bruised, our hands lacerated; sleepless, hungry; our temples racked by pain, our nostrils choked with sand, our limbs stiffened and bent with cramps; but after rinsing our mouths and dipping our heads in some little creek, the water of which we dare not drink, and pushing on three or four miles ahead of the stage, winding up the long prairie swells, and breathing the morning air, we pause in our brisk step, look at each other, and smile. The effect is magical; all pain, all cramp, all languor, have disappeared; the blood flows freely, the lungs act softly, the nostrils seem to open from within, and the eyes appear to cast out sand and dust by some internal force. If we could only now get food, we feel strength enough to defy all other forms of pain.

But food is a thing we cannot get.

CHAPTER V.

Prairie Indians.

The red-men of these Prairies have been taking counsel together in a field near Fort Ellsworth, as to the policy of allowing the white men, headed by their Big Father in Washington, to open a new road through their country by way of this Smoky Hill Fork; and the warlike tribes of this region, the Cheyennes and Arappahoes, aided and supported by allies from the south and from the north, the powerful Sioux, the savage Kiowas, the clever Comanches, and the swift Apaches, are said to have resolved on war.

These Indians say they have been deceived by the white men; this they always say when going out on the war-path; for a red man's pride will not suffer him to acknowledge, even to himself, that he has done any wrong — that he has broken any pledge. In these frontier quarrels, the Indian, by his own confession, is always right. So far as we can learn from these Cheyennes and their allies, it would seem that early in the spring of this present year (1866) Major Wyncoop, an officer of government, employed in the task of making treaties — a brisk and profitable branch of the public service — had been among these prairie hunters, giving them arms and blankets, flour and whisky, in exchange for a promise of good behaviour on the roads in respect to emigrant waggons and merchants' trains. Wyncoop, they say, had told them, by word of mouth, to have no fears about the safety of their buffalo-runs, since the Big Father in Washington had no intention of opening any new road by way of the Smoky Hill. After Wyncoop left them, they began to fear that he had been a bearer of lies; for they heard that, even while he was sleeping in their lodge, eating elk with Roman Nose, Black Hawk, and Spotted Dog, Cheyenne chiefs and warriors, the white men had been laying their plans for cutting a road straight towards the heart of these buffalo lands.

Of course they have heard from the Pale-faces that all roads should be free and open. They have been told that the road from St. Louis to New York is just as free to a red man as to a white man; and they have been also told, as though this second thing followed from the first, that the path from St. Louis to Salt Lake should be as free to the white man as it is to the red; but Roman Nose, Black Hawk, and Spotted Dog, are men too subtle to be taken in by what they call baby-talk. They answer, that in their sense of the word yon road from St. Louis to New York is not open. Would Black Hawk be allowed to hunt through the fields of Ohio? Would Spotted Dog be suffered to pitch his lodge in the streets of Indianapolis? Could Roman Nose, on that road from St. Louis to New York, kill and eat sheep and cow, animals which have replaced his own buffalo and elk? If not, how, they ask, can the track be called open to them, dwellers in wigwams, hunters of wild game? These Cheyennes, these Arappahoes and Sioux, are as well aware as any pale-face in Washington, that their laws are not our laws, their liberties not our liberties. If it were one of their Indian fashions to have a party-cry, they would probably raise the shout of "The hunting-ground for the hunter!"

Roman Nose and Spotted Dog tell us that the very best hunting-grounds now left to the red man, are these prairie lands, lying along and around the Smoky Hill Fork; a dry and sandy ravine, more than a hundred miles in length, stretching at the foot of this high ridge or bluff, called Smoky Hill from the cap of mist which commonly floats above its crest. Here grow the sweet bunch-grasses which the buffalo loves to chew, and hither come those herds of game on which the Indian lodge depends for its winter store. Disturb these herds in their present quarters, and whither can they flee? Southward lies the Arkansas road from St. Louis to Santa Fé; northward lies the Platte road from Omaha to Salt Lake. No game will linger on the white man's track; and to make a path for the mail by way of Smoky Hill Fork is simply to drive away the red man's food. Elk and antelope may wander into close vicinity to a trader's and an emigrant's trail; buffalo, a bolder and fiercer, but more cautious animal, never.

"White man come, buffalo go," says Black Hawk, with his sharp logic; "when buffalo gone, squaw and papoose die."

From Black Hawk's point of view, the policy of

resisting our encroachments on their hunting-fields is beyond dispute.

A second cause has helped to create the trouble which besets us on these Plains.

One of the great feuds which divide Eastern America from Western America — the states lying east of the Mississippi from the states and territories lying west of the Big Drink — has its birth in the question — What line of policy should be followed by the government in dealing with the red men? The Eastern cities are all for rose-water and baby-talk; the Western cities are all for revolvers and bowie-knives. Each section has its sentiment and its passion. In Boston no one believes that a red Indian can do wrong; in Denver no one believes that a red Indian can do right. Each party accuses the other of ignorance and petulance; Massachusetts looking on the red-skin solely in his romantic lights, as a representative of tribes and nations, dear to art and poetry, which are rapidly passing into the land of dreams; Colorado looking upon him solely in his prosaic aspects of a thief, a beggar, an assassin, who may have stolen white women and scalped white men. In Massachusetts, in Rhode Island, in New Hampshire, almost everybody has either made a sketch, composed a song, or read a romance, about the Indian; while in Colorado, in New Mexico and California, almost everybody has had a kinsman butchered or a kinswoman carried off by that romantic personage: — a difference which may very well account for the radical opposition of ideas as to a true Indian policy in the East and in the West.

Being strong in Washington, Massachusetts has commonly had her own way in Kansas, and wherever else a judge's writ will run; being near to the Plains, Colorado has sometimes had her own way in the lonely grass land and the nameless creek.

One sudden blow Colorado dealt last year at her savage enemy, when a body of volunteer horse under Colonel Shevington broke into a Cheyenne camp at Sand Creek, a little way in our front, where a thousand Indians had encamped, under the command of White Antelope, an aged and renowned Cheyenne warrior. The Colorado volunteers, raised by orders from Washington, rode in upon these Indians, shooting down brave, and squaw, and papoose, in undistinguishing hate and wrath. White Antelope fell like the hero in a poet's tale; for, seeing that defence was idle, that escape was impossible, he sprang up a mound of sand, and throwing open his embroidered jacket, bade the Pale-faces fire. With twenty slugs in his body, he rolled upon the earth. Most of his followers fell around his corpse; old and young, men and women, wrinkled warriors and puling infants. Sixteen of the volunteers were slain; and their comrades rode back into Denver covered, as they imagined, with the glory of their deed.

In New England, this raid upon the Cheyenne camp is everywhere denounced as the Indian Massacre; in the ranches of these prairies, in the cities near the mines, it is everywhere celebrated as the Big Fight. Your opinion on the point is held to be a test of your good sense. In Boston, any approval of the big fight would subject you to a social ban; in Denver, any denunciation of the Indian massacre would bring a bowie-knife into your side. After saying so much, I need scarcely add, that westward of the Missouri I have never met a man who does not say that the Sand Creek affair, though terrible enough in some of its details, was a good and wholesome act of severity, — an act that ought to be repeated twice a-year, until every Indian tribe has been swept away from these Plains.

Eastern men assert, that when Shevington attacked the Indian camp, the Cheyennes were at peace with the whites, and that the American flag was floating above White Antelope's tent. Shevington denies these facts; asserting that the Cheyenne camp had been the refuge of Dog soldiers, a band of red-skin outlaws and assassins, who had been plundering settlements, and murdering teamsters and emigrants for many months; a fact which he and his Colorado friends assert was proved: in the first place, by the Indians having had a white girl, of sixteen, and three young white children in that very camp, whom they sold, after much palaver, to the citizens: in the second place, by their boast of having two other white women in their lodges, whom they would neither give away nor sell: in the third place, by the white men finding, when the Indian camp was taken, a heap of rings, ribbons, photographs, and human scalps.

One act of atrocity, committed by these Indians, is said to have roused, in a peculiar manner, the indignation of Denver. In a ranch, on Running Creek, near that city, lived, with his wife and two children, a man named Hungate; an honest man, a good farmer, who stood well with his neighbours. The red men had swept down upon his lonely farm, had driven off his cattle, had burnt his ranch, had violated his wife, had massacred his children, and shot himself. The heads of all the Hungate family were scalped, the bodies hacked and pounded. When they were found in this mutilated state, they had been borne into Denver city, and made a public show, like the wounded men of Paris in '48; rousing the hot blood of Colorado into madness.

White Antelope was made to answer for the blood of Hungate.

Two of the scalps which the volunteers under Shevington found at Sand Creek, after the fight, are said to have been fresh; one, a white man's scalp, was hardly cold; a second, a white woman's scalp, was declared by the army surgeon to have been drawn within ten days.

Feud begets feud, and the strife of last year can only be answered by strife in the coming fall. A son of White Antelope is now going about the Plains calling on the tribes and nations to rise and avenge his father's death; which Roman Nose, Black Hawk, Tall Buffalo, Lance, and Little Blanket, all powerful chiefs, are said to be willing enough to do, since they may gain a rare opportunity of gratifying their passion for blood while clearing these favourite buffalo-runs of all white disturbers of the Indian game.

CHAPTER VI.

The Red Man.

A LONG line of poems and novels leads an English reader into habits of looking on the red man as a picturesque figure of the prairie and the lake, rather than as a living force in the midst of American cities. We have lodged the Indians in our minds, as we have the men who exist for us only in tales and plays. When we recall either an Iroquois, or a Mohican, he presents himself to our vision in his war-paint, in his hunting gear; he is sitting in council under the Treaty tree, seeing God in clouds, and hearing Him in the wind. We note him stealing forth with Hawk-eye on the war-path, watching over Minnehaha in the wigwam, tearing himself from his old hunting-grounds on the Ohio, starting for his new home in the unknown West. We connect him with aged hemlocks, running waters, and silent valleys. But whether he comes before us in his hunting gear or in his paint and feathers, with a pipe of peace in his mouth or a scalping-knife raised in his hand, he is ever the same for us; a being of the mind, a picture, a poem, a romance; not a man of flesh and blood, endowed with senses, rich in passions, fruitful in ideas, one strong to resist, one swift to impress, all men who may come into contact with him.

In the United States people know him better. The red man lives amongst them like the black man; less ductile in genius, more prolific in ideas; having his own policy, his own arts, his own traditions; with a power, which the black man has not, of giving back, no less than taking, in the way of thought. They have to deal with him from day to day as with a man having rights in the soil which no Yankee can deny, which no honest Yankee feels the wish to dispute.

No race of men ever yet drove out another race of men from any country, taking their lands and cities from them, without finding on the spot which they came to own a local genius, which affected their polity, their usages and their arts. Man is a living power, acting and re-acting on his fellow, through a natural law. All force is relative. If the strong act upon the weak, the weak re-act upon the strong. Numbers are strength; and if the higher race should have the disadvantage of being few in number, they will fall in some measure to the level of their slaves, in spite of their first superiority in physical gifts and in moral power. Thus, the Roman masters of Greece adopted the art, the language, the religion, and at length the country, they had won by the sword. The Norman hero became an English gentleman, helping to make that name the proudest title borne on earth. After three generations, the settlers under Strongbow proved themselves more Irish in feeling, than the Celts. Duke Rollo's soldiers softened into Sicilians. The Mantchoo Tartars have become Chinese. Even in cases where fire and sword have been used to thin off the original people, the effect has been, pretty much the same. The Israelites were told to cut down the Hittites and Amorites, the Canaanites, Perizzites and Jebusites; and they slew the men of these nations without mercy, as they had been commanded from God. Yet the customs and ideas of these heathens clung to the soil, and generation after generation of the chosen people fell into sin by running after the native gods. Dagon, Moloch, Ashtaroth, drew men away from Jehovah; and the arts of Tyre and Sidon acted upon those whom the sword of Jabin could not drive from the land. In like fashion, those red men whom our fore-comers found on the Atlantic sea-board, and whom they have been pushing back, at first towards the Alleghanies, then to the Ohio and the Wabash, afterwards to the Mississippi, and at length beyond the great river as far west as the Kansas and the Arkansas, have left the traces of their former presence in the national mind; in the popular politics, in the popular science, in the popular life. They have done so in places from which they have wholly disappeared, as well perhaps as in districts where they still exist; among the Spiritualists of New England, among the Mormons of Salt Lake valley. Man is what he eats; and a nation grows into the likeness of that which it absorbs. Where the Indian has been destroyed by assimilation, the pale-face must have undergone a change, to be measured by the amount of resisting power; a quality in which some tribes of these red-skins are pre-eminently rich. When the Indian has survived the shock of conflict with the pale-face, as at Oneida Creek, at Wyandotte, at St. Mary's Mission, and in many other places, the power of acting and re-acting on the whites is still in force, affecting the national character in a way which no man could have foreseen, and no one will now deny.

The Anglo-Saxon power of assimilation is very great; but the Cheyenne and the Dakota present to it, perhaps, the very hardest meal it has ever been called upon to digest. The Anglo-Saxon has not gone far in the process of eating up the red man; yet he shows by a hundred signs the effect of that indigestible meal upon his health. The Indian fibre is exceedingly tough. Can any one say whether, up to this moment, though the white men have an easy mastery, the action of the white men on the red has been stronger than that of the red men on the white?

Let those who think so come into these western plains, into the lands where red and white men live together, in anything but harmony. They will find that each has acquired the other's vices; that while the Indian has learned how to beat his pale brother in debauchery, the white man has only come to equal his red brother in ferocity and craft. If the Yengee has taught the Indian to drink whisky, the Indian has taught the Yengee to keep squaws. Nearly all the old trappers and teamsters, who have lived among Indians, are polygamists:— Jem Baker, of Clear Creek, has two squaws: Mageary, of South Platte, has three; Bent, of Smoky Hill, is said to have married six. As an Indian chief said to Colonel

Marcy, "The first thing a Yengee wants in the Plains is plenty wife." If Little Bear drinks and beats his squaw to death, Jem Smithers has learned to make a jest of taking scalps. I hear anecdotes in these plains to make the blood run cold. Jack Dunkier, of Central City, scalped five Sioux in the presence of his white comrade. The same Colorado boy is said to have ridden into Denver with the leg of an Indian warrior slung to his saddle; a leg which he had cut from the trunk, and on which he reported that he had been living for two whole days. No one believed his story; but a boast is in its way a fact, and there is no doubt that in Denver city a white man openly boasted of having boiled and eaten steaks from a human thigh. A Pawnee would glory in such a deed; vaunting it afterwards in the meetings of his tribe. The Yengee quickly learns to imitate the red man's crimes. One of the Sand Creek volunteers returned to Denver with a woman's heart on the head of a pole; having shot the squaw, ripped her breast open, and plucked out her heart. No one blamed him, and his trophy was received with shouts by a rabble in the public streets. I am glad to say, that white opinion underwent a change, even in the rough mining districts, with respect to this man's doings; not that any one dreamed of arresting him for his crimes, not that his comrades in the ranks thought any worse of him for his lark; but the jokes of the grog-shop, the gaming-house, and the smoking-room, turned rather freely on his deed, and the fellow, being deficient in wit and patience, fled away from the town, and never came back. In a Cheyenne brave, such a crime as his would have raised a warrior to the rank of a chief. One offence, though it implied no loss of life, appeared to me more revolting than even the murder of a squaw in war time — the violation of Indian graves by Yengees. A government train, passing through the Indian territory, came upon a heap of stones and rocks, which the knowing trapper who accompanied the train pointed out as the burial-place of some great chief: when the western boys ripped it open, kicked the bones of the dead warrior, and picked up the bow and arrows, the spoon of buffalo horn, (an officer of the United States army gave me that horn as a keepsake!) the beads and ornaments, the remnants of a buffalo robe in which the chief had been wrapped for his final rest.

Along with many of their vices, the Yengees have borrowed from the Indians some of their simple virtues — a spirit of hospitality, a high respect for the plighted word, a sovereign contempt for pain and death.

The red men have taught the whole world how to smoke the Indian weed. Have they received from the Pale-face any one boon to compare with this gift from the savage to the civilised man?

It is no figure of speech to say that in White America, a red influence is very widely spread and very strongly felt, alike in the sphere of institutions and in the sphere of thought.

The confederacy of the Five Nations was the type adopted by the whites when framing the confederacy of the Thirteen Colonies; not only as regards the principle of their Union, but also in respect to its most original details. The Iroquois had invented the theory of State Rights, which the colonists borrowed from them; an indefinable and dangerous theory, implying a power of separate action, perhaps of withdrawal, from the Union; leading to a thousand quarrels, and to a civil war, of which the end has not yet been reached. These Iroquois had adopted the theory of extending their power and territory, not by adding to the limits of any existing nation of the confederacy, but by bodily introducing new tribes and nations into union; a novel principle of political growth, which the white men also borrowed from them. Under these two principles, the Five Nations had grown into Eight Nations; and the Thirteen Colonies, following in their wake and carrying on their work, have expanded into Forty-six States and Territories.

In the conference of 1774, when commissioners from Pennsylvania, Maryland, and Virginia, went to consult the Iroquois sachems at Lancaster, the great chief Casannatego addressed them in terms which a Greek member of the Achaian League might have used: "Our wise forefathers established union and amity between the Five Nations. This union has made us formidable. This has given us great strength and authority with our neighbouring nations. By showing the same method, you will acquire fresh strength and power. Therefore, I counsel you, whatever befalls you, never to fall out with one another." Official reports to Congress from the Indian bureau confess that this Iroquois confederation was the true political germ of the United States.

The men of the Five Nations had very high notions of liberty, and that on both the public and the domestic side. Every man was considered equal to his fellow. The sachem, even when he came of a ruling stock, was elected to his office. They had no hereditary rank, and no other titles than the names which described their function, such as warrior, councillor, and seer. They said that all men of Iroquois race, together with their allies, were born free and equal with each other; and that no man, thus freely born, could ever be made a slave. Indeed, they set their faces against slavery in any form. No Iroquois could own his fellow. If enemies were taken by him in war, they were either put to death or naturalised and adopted into his tribe. Nay, the sentiment of freedom was so strong in the Five Nations that they declared the soil itself free, so that no slave could be found within the districts hunted by these red-men, even when negro slaves were everywhere being bought and sold in the streets of Boston, Philadelphia, and New York. In time, however, some of the less noble tribes of Indians — Cherokees, Choktaws, and Chickasaws — learned from the white men to buy and to steal their negro brother, and to hold him in bondage, like a mule or a dog.

Among many of the Indian tribes, though less in these savage western provinces than among the Delawares, Mohicans, and Senecas, the women have a singular degree of power; not only in the wigwam, where they occupy the seats of honour, but in public places and in public life; even the right of holding meetings and discussing questions of peace and war. Among the higher class of Indian tribes, the braves take a pride in paying to their squaws a measure of respect exceeding the mere courtesies of city life; often rising into what, for lack of a better name, might be called chivalry; a fine feeling of the strong towards the weak, as such; a softening of the hard towards the gentle; a bending of the warrior towards the hus-wife. Of course, in a settled society, where rights are guarded by law, not left to the caprice of individual will, there should be little need for this open and avowed protection, on the part of men towards women. It is a virtue of the savage and the semi-savage, of the hunter and the herdsman, of the Seneca Indian and the Anezi Arab; which has not failed to touch with moral and poetic beauty the manners of a people of far nobler grade.

What man can doubt that Indian ideas on witchcraft, on polygamy, on plurality of gods, on the migration of souls, on the presence of spirits, on future rewards, have entered deeply into the popular mind, and are now affecting for good or ill the course of American religious thought?

One of the first things to strike an English eye about these red-skins (after their paint and feathers, perhaps), is their division into tribes; the oldest form in which men were organised into societies. It is an Oriental system; found in Media and India, in Arabia and Scythia, among all the wandering and pastoral nations. In the first step from savage towards civil life, all races are divided into tribes, of either the family or the clan. In Sparta there were three of these original tribes, in Athens four, in Palestine twelve, in Rome three; in each of which states one tribe would appear to have had some sort of regal superiority: the Hyllean at Sparta, the Eupatrid in Athens, the house of Judah in Palestine, the Ramnes in Rome. Among these multitudinous tribes of the red race, no such regal character appears to obtain; the Cheyenne admits no moral superiority in the Sioux, the Mohican in the Seneca; each nation is a separate body; and the chief policy of the red natives is that of maintaining their tribal independence. From them the white settlers have borrowed the sentiment of State rights.

CHAPTER VII.

Indian Life.

The story of Minnehaha, Laughing Water, has made known the fact that there exists, among these sons of the lake and prairie, a body of tradition available for art. The life of a Red Indian — as he starts on a trail, as he hunts the bison and the elk, as he courts his mistress with the scalp of an enemy slain in battle, or by stealth, as he leaps in the wardance, as he buries the hatchet and lays by the knife, as he harangues his fellows in council, as he defies the malice of his captors, as he sits down under his hemlock and smokes the pipe of peace — is nothing less than a romance. His presence is a picture, his conduct a poem. The forest in which he dwells, the plain on which he hunts, the river along which he floats, are full to him of a myriad spirits. His canoe is an ark, his wigwam is a tent. On every side he is in contact with the innermost soul of things, and nature speaks to his ear out of every leaf and from every stone. What marvel, then, that his unwritten poetry should be of a wild and daring kind; new in its character, fresh in its colours, like and yet unlike to the Homeric, the Ossianic, and the Gothic primitive romance?

A young hunter fell in love with a beautiful girl whom he sought for his wife, and being the pride of his tribe, both for swiftness in the race and for courage in war, his suit was accepted by her father, and she was given to him in marriage. On her wedding-day she died. Tearing a trench in the soil, the women swathed her limbs in a cloth, and after wailing over her body, laid her down in the bunch-grass. But the young hunter could not leave her. His bow was unstrung in the wigwam, his club lay idle on the ground, for his heart was buried in that forest grave, and his ears were no longer awake to the sounds of war and the chase. One joy was left to him on earth: — to sit by himself, near that mound under which his love lay at rest, pondering of his lost bride, and following her in fancy to the spirit-land. Old men of the tribe had told him, when a child, that souls go after death to the Blessed Isles, lying far off to the south, in a sunny clime, upon the bosom of a placid lake, under a sky of unfreckled blue; and one day, as he sat on the cold ground, with snow in the trees above him, the thought came into his mind that he would go in search of that Island in which the soul of his mistress dwelt. Turning his face to the south, he began his journey, which, for a long while, lay through a country of lakes, hills, valleys, much like his own; but in time there appeared to be less snow in the trees, less frost on the streams, more brightness in the air, more verdure on the earth; then he came upon buds and blossoms, he saw flowers in the field, and heard warblings in the bush. Seeing a path into a thick grove, he followed it through the trees until it led him to a high ridge, on the top of which stood an Indian lodge. At the door of this lodge, an old man, with white hair, a pale face, and fiery eyes, covered with skins of wild beasts, and leaning on a staff, received him with a sad smile. The hunter was beginning to tell his story: — "Hush!" said the old man; "I expected you, and have risen to give you welcome. She whom you seek has been here; she rested for awhile, and then went on. Come into my lodge." When the hunter was refreshed with food and sleep, the old man led him forth of the lodge and said: "See you that gulf and the plain beyond? It is the land of souls. You stand upon its confines, and my lodge is the gate of entry. But only souls can pass beyond this gate. Lay down your bundle and your quiver; leave behind your body and your dog; now, pass into the land of spirits." The hunter bounded from the earth, like a bird on its wings. Forest, lake, mountain, were the same, but he saw them with new eyes, and felt them with a strange touch. Nature seemed to have become luminous and vocal. The air was softer, the sky was brighter, the sward was greener, than they seem to our mortal senses. Birds sang to him out of trees, and animals came frisking past him. No creature was afraid of him, for blood is never shed in the spirit-land. He went forward without effort, gliding, rather than walking, along the ground; passing through trees and rocks as a man in the flesh might walk through a wreath of spray and a cloud of smoke. At length he came to a wide and shining lake, from the midst of which sprang a lovely isle. A canoe of white stone lay close in shore, with paddles laid ready to his hand. Stepping into this boat, and pushing from the bank, he became conscious, as in a dream, that another white canoe was at his side, in which, pale and beautiful as he had last seen her, sat his bride. As he put forth from the bank, she put off also; answering to the motion of his oars like the chords in music. A tranquil joy was in the hunter's heart as they pushed their way towards the Blessed Isle. On looking forward towards the land, he was seized with fear for his beloved; a great white line of surf broke angrily in their front, and in the clear deep waters he could see the bodies of drowning men and the bones of thousands who had perished in that surf. His thews being strong and his courage calm, he had no fears for himself; but he yearned for her, exposed to the surf in that glittering shell; but when they pushed boldly into the breakers, they found their canoes go through them as through air. Around them were many boats, each freighted with a soul. Some were in sore distress, some wrecked and lost. The boats which bore young children glided home like birds. Those containing youths and maidens met with gusts and rollers. Older men were beaten by storms and tempests, each according to his deeds; for the calm and storm were not in the spirit-lake, but in the men who sailed upon it. Softly running to the shore, the hunter and his bride leaped lightly from their canoes upon the Golden Isle. What a change from the dull, cold earth on which the hunter lived! They saw no graves. They never heard of war. No gales ever vexed the air, no fogs ever hid the sun. Ice was unknown to that Blessed Isle. No blood was ever shed; no hunger and thirst were felt; for the very air which they breathed was food and drink. Their feet were never tired and their temples never ached. No sorrowing was endured for the dead. Gladly would the hunter have remained for ever with his bride in this spirit-land; but a great presence, called the Master of Life, came near to him, and speaking in a voice like a soft breeze, said to the young man: — "Go back to the land from which you came; your day is not yet. Return to your tribe, and to the duty of a good man. When that is done, you will rejoin the spirit which you love. She is accepted; she will be here for ever; as young, as happy as when I called her from the land of snow." When the voice ceased from its speaking, the hunter started in his sleep — to find the little mound at his feet, snow in the trees overhead, and a numb sorrow in his heart.

Ah me, it was all a dream!

The red man believes in a god, or rather, he believes in many gods; also in a life after death, to be shared by his horse, his hawk, and his dog. He thinks there is a good spirit and a bad spirit, equal in dignity and strength to each other; that, under them, live a multitude of gods; spirits of the rock, the tree, the cloud, the river, and the frost; spirits of the wind, of the sun, and of the stars. No Greek shepherd ever peopled Hymettus and Arcadia, Orion and the Bear, with such swarming multitudes of shapes and radiances as the Cheyenne, the Pawnee, and the Snake, believe to inhabit their plains and mountains, their creeks and woods, their lakes and skies. But the Indian has never yet learned to erect temples to his deities; being content to find them in tree and flower, in sunshine and in storm, in the hawk, the beaver, and the trout. His only religion is that of nature, his only worship a kind of magic. He believes in witches and in sorcerers; in their power to degrade men into beasts, to elevate beasts into men. Sleep is to him but another side of his life, and dreams are as real as his waking deeds. In his fancy all space is teeming with gods and spirits, which are close to him as he hunts and fights, capable of hearing his call to them, of making known to him their presence and their wishes by signs and sounds. He is the original source of all our spirit-rapping, all our table-turning; and in the act of invoking demons to his aid, he is still beyond the reach of such puny rivals as the Davenports and Homes.

His religious rites are few and cabalistic; thus, he will sing for the sick, and offer meat to the dead; he will put a charm in his ear, in his nose, and around his wrist — commonly a shell from the great sea — as a defence against evil spirits. He has no priest, as we understand the word, but he submits himself abjectly to his prophet (jossakeed) and seer; and he does so, not only as regards his soul, but his body. In fact, his prophet is his doctor also; disease being in his opinion a spiritual as well as physical defect, only to be conquered by one who has power upon sin and death. Brigham Young has very much the same function to perform at one end of Salt

Lake that a Shoshonee seer may have to discharge at the other.

The red men have no settled laws. Their government is patriarchal, the chief power being exercised, as in every savage horde, by the old men of the tribe, except in war time, when the bravest and most cunning take the lead. They know nothing about votes, either free or open, but in electing leaders they declare their preference with a shout. They have no conception of the use and power of work, and it is only with a slow and sullen heart that even the best among them will consent to practise a trade. They have about them a sense of having always been a wild tribe; a race of hunters and warriors, lords of the arrow and the club; and they are too proud to moil and toil, to do the offices of squaws and cowards. If they were not driven by hunger to the chase, they would do nothing at all, except drink and fight. In these things the Creeks and the Dakotas excel the most accomplished rowdies of Denver, Leavenworth, and New York.

I cannot say that their domestic life is either noble or lovely. A prairie brave, mounted on a strong pony, with a rifle on his saddle, a blanket strapped behind him, dressed in a handsome skin jacket, adorned with beads and tags, with his squaw trudging heavily by his side on foot, carrying her papoose on her back, and a parcel of provisions in her hands, was one of my earliest illustrations of the chivalries of Indian life. A mob of Ute warriors, tearing through the streets of Denver, rushing into shops and painting their faces, while the squaws and papooses tumbled after them in the mire, laden with cabbages, buffalo-skins, and miscellaneous domestic fry, was another. A listless, insolent crowd of Pawnees, smoking and drinking on the Pacific road, while their squaws were labouring on the railway line as navvies, hired out by the braves at fifty cents a-day, and a ration of corn and meat uncooked, was a third. As such examples grew in strength upon me, I began to think the noble Indian was not so much of a gentleman as a believing reader of the Last of the Mohicans might suppose. "Why don't these fellows work for themselves, instead of lounging in groceries and grog-shops, while their wives are digging earth and carrying wood?" An Omaha friend who stood near me smiled: — "Don't you see, they are warriors and gentlemen; they cannot degrade themselves by work."

The Sioux, the Pawnee, the Cheyenne squaw, though she may have a certain power in the wigwam, and an uncertain liberty of speech in the council, when her character as a woman happens to be great, is, in many respects, and as a general rule, no better than a slave; such rights as she may exercise belonging to her rather as a member of the tribe than as a mother and a wife. Her husband has probably bought her for a blanket, for an old carbine, for a keg of whisky; and it depends wholly on the man's humour, on his fondness, whether he shall treat her as a lady or as a dog. He can sell her, he can give her away. The squaw's inferiority to the hunter is like that of the horse to his master. She is one of the man's chattels; one of many like herself; for the

Indian is a polygamist, and keeps a harem in the prairie. She has to perform all in-door, all out-door labour; to fix the wigwam in the ground, to fetch water from the stream, to gather billets from the bush, to dig roots and pick up acorns, to dress and cook the food, to make the clothes, to dry the scalps, to mend the wigwam, to carry her children on the march. And while she has a thousand toils to endure, she has scarcely any rights as either a woman or a wife. The man may put her away for the most trifling fault. Her infant may be taken from her lap. Her modesty is not always spared. While the sins into which her own fancies may have led her are visited with revolting punishment, she may be forced by her husband into acts of immorality which degrade her as a woman, not only in her own eyes, but in those of the companions of her shame. If she commits adultery without her husband's leave, his custom allows him to slit her nose; yet when the whimsy takes him, he may sell her charms to a passing guest. In the freedom of his forest life, it is common for the Shoshonee and the Comanche to offer his squaw to any stranger visiting in his lodge. The theory of the wigwam is, that the female member of it is a chattel, and that her beauty, her modesty, her service, belong to her lord only, and may be given as he lists. For her there is nothing save to hear and to obey.

And the Indian squaw is what such rules of life must make her. If her mate is cruel in disposition, she is savage; if he is dirty in person, she is filthy; if he is lax in conduct, she is shameless. When anything base and monstrous has to be done, it is left to the squaws. If an enemy is to be tortured, the women are set upon him. A brave might club his prisoner to death by a blow, but the sharper and slower agonies caused by peeling off his skin, by tearing out his nails, by breaking his finger-joints, by putting fire under his feet, by gouging out his eyes, are only to be inflicted by the demons who have taken up their dwelling in female forms.

All the men who fought against the Indians at Sand Creek, to whom I have spoken, describe the squaws as fighting more furiously than the braves; and all the white women (as I hear) who have had the double misfortune of falling into Indian hands, and surviving to tell the tale of their dishonour, exclaim against the squaws as deeper in cruelty and iniquity than their lords. The story of a white woman's captivity among the Sioux and Arappahoes is one that ought never to be told. In Colorado there are fifty, perhaps a hundred, females who have undergone the shame of such a passage in their lives; and it is fearful to see the flashing eyes, to hear the emphatic oaths, of either father, son, or lover to one of these wretched creatures, when a Cheyenne is spoken of otherwise than as a dog, whom it is the duty of every honest man to shoot.

It would be a dangerous trial for a Yengee to say one word in favour of the Indians either in the streets of Denver and Central City, or along the route through the Rocky Mountains travelled by the waggon trains and the mail.

Yet with all their faults, the Indians have some

virtues and many capacities. They are brave. As a rule they are chaste. In patience they have few equals; in endurance they have none. They are affectionate towards their children; moderately faithful to their squaws. Their reverence for age, for wisdom, and for valour, is akin to religious feeling, and is only a little lower in degree than that which they pay to their Great Spirit. In war time, and against an enemy, they consider everything fair; but the first and worst of all vices in the savage, the habit of lying, is comparatively rare in these red men.

CHAPTER VIII.

Carrying the Mail.

IN bands from fifteen to forty, well armed and well mounted, the Cheyennes and their allies are moving along our line, plundering the stations, threatening the teamsters and drivers with fire and lead. A red-skin war is never sudden in its coming; for, as many tribes and nations must be drawn into it, there is much running to and fro, much smoking of tobacco, and a vast amount of palaver. When a man desires to have war, he must first persuade his chief and his tribe to dare it; next he must ride round the country into other tribes, whispering, haranguing, rousing, till the blood of many of the younger braves boils up. Meetings must be held, counsels compared, and a decision taken by the allies. If the palavering, in which the aged and timid warriors have a principal share, is going on slowly, some of the younger braves steal off into the enemy's land, where they provoke bad blood by plundering a ranch, driving away mules, if possible carrying off women. They know that the white men will turn out and fight, that two or three braves may happen to get killed, and they are pretty sure that the nations which have suffered in the fray will then cry loudly for revenge.

As a rule, the white men, being few in number,

unsupported by their government, never resist these Indian attacks, unless life is taken or women are captured; short of these crimes being committed, the pale-face says, it is cheaper to feed the red men than to fight them, since he must always meet them with a halter round his neck. A white man dare not fire on a band of Comanches, though he may be perfectly sure that they are enemies, bent on taking his life. If he killed an Indian, he would be tried for murder. The red man, therefore, has his choice of when and where he will attack; and the grand advantage of being able to deliver his volley when he pleases. It is only after some one has been killed, that the white man feels himself safe in returning shot for shot. So, when parties of Indians come upon lonely ranches and stations on the Plains, the white men have to kill, as it were, the fatted calf, — that is to say, they have to bring forth their stores of bacon, dried buffalo tongue, beans, and potted fruit, set the kettle boiling, the pan frying, and feed the rascals who are going to murder them, down to the very last pound of flesh, the very last crust of bread; only too happy if they will then go away into their wilds without taking away women and scalps. Of course, few women are to be found in these perilous plains; not a dozen between Wamego and Denver, I should say.

Now these small bands of Cheyennes and Arappahoes in our front have come from the great camp of the Six Nations, lying near Fort Ellsworth, under the command of Roman Nose. They are going forward as a party of feelers and provokers, a little way in advance of us, insulting the whites, and eating up the road. At every station, after passing Fort Riley, we hear of their presence and of their depredations.

Red skins, however, will not permit themselves to be seen, unless they are friendly and mean to beg. In going over one of the long, low ridges of Smoky Hill, we observe a small party of Cheyennes moving along the opposite ridge; they are mounted, and leading spare horses; and as we catch the gleam of their rifles, we know they are well armed. Unlike the Bedouin, every red-skin has a revolver of his own; some of them have two or three revolvers in their belts; almost every one slings a rifle across his horse. They seem to be crossing our path. "Who are these Indians?" I ask the driver, by whose side I am sitting on the box. "Well," says he, in the deliberate Western fashion, "guess they are some cuss." They seem to have halted; for the moment, as I think, they are trying to prevent our seeing a white horse, which one of them is leading. "Guess I can't make them out," adds the driver, after taking time to consider his want of opinion; "if they were friendly, they would come to us and beg; if they were thieves, they would hide in the creek, so as not to be seen; guess they are out on the war-path." When they draw up, we can count them; they are only five men in number, with four led horses in addition to their own. Five men would not dream of attacking the mail, in which there might be a dozen men and guns; especially not when the blinds are down, and they cannot from their coign of vantage see into the coach, and count the number of their foes. A sure knowledge of the enemies to be met in fight is a cardinal point in the system of an Indian warrior, who prides himself more on his success than even on his valour. Rich in stratagem, he is always afraid of ambuscade; and he rarely ventures to attack an enemy, when, from either want of light or any other cause, he cannot see into every element of his game.

This Indian fact is of use to us now. In the presence of our Cheyenne neighbours, we draw the curtains of our waggon pretty close; so that the red-skins, who can see that we are two outside, the driver and myself, cannot tell how many more may be sitting inside with revolvers. They know in a general way that no one rides outside the stage in the burning heat of these plains, unless the inside seats are filled. The rule is not good for us, our seats being occupied with mail-bags; but the Cheyennes and Comanches have no notice of our straits. Now, five red-skins, though they might rush upon a single man, or even upon a couple of men, no better armed than themselves, against whom they would enjoy the privilege of firing the first volley, will always pause before pulling a trigger on a foe of invisible and unknown strength. It is, therefore, without surprise, though with much inward satisfaction, that we see them break up their council, fall into line, and move along the creek, in such a way as to increase the distance between us at every stride.

At the next log-hut, we find that this party of Cheyennes, with the led horses, — stolen from some waggon train, — have been here; very insolent and masterly; not mincing words; not concealing threats. They have eaten up everything in the station; the dried elk, the buffalo-tongue, the fat bacon, the canned fruits; have compelled the boys to boil them coffee, to fetch clean water, to mend their horses' shoes; and have left the place with a notice that the mail must be stopped, the stock removed, and the shanties burnt.

Having tasted a little putrid water, seasoned with a few drops of cognac, happily carried from New York, we push out of the station, following in the track of these menacing braves. We crash through ravines, in which our driver believes they lurk; and we pass little mounds, under which the scalpless heads of white men, murdered in the recent frays, have scarcely yet grown cold. The long green line of the Smoky Hill is on our left, not half a mile from our course, which lies for two or three days and nights along the bank of Smoky river. As we dash into Low Creek, we find the men in a scare, though they are only a few miles distant from Ellsworth. A party of Cheyennes have been to the station, have eaten up their food, have taken away what they wanted, and promised to return in fifteen days, to burn down the shanty and murder the men. The boys say these Indians will come back before the end of their fifteen days. They notice many signs of the red man's anger, which are invisible to us. The blacksmith went out in the morning; but he saw enough in an hour to induce him to scamper back. A farmer, living in a ranch close by, has called in his man and horses from the plains. Every one is belted and on guard; in all, five men against as many thousand red-skins. With some satisfaction, we hear of seven United States soldiers, from the fort, having ridden on in front of us, looking after buffalo and red-skins. The mules having been yoked, our revolvers fired off and reloaded, and a can of bad water swallowed, we light our cigars and jump on the waggon.

Just as we are sallying from the station, a riderless horse comes sweating and panting into the yard, and is instantly recognised as belonging to one of those soldiers who had passed through in the early day, looking after buffalo and red-skins. One or other he seems to have found. Bill the driver pulls at his reins, doubtful whether he ought to go out; but on second thoughts, with an ugly twist of the jaw and resolute scowl on his brow, he whips his team into a rage, and plunges out with them upon the hot and arid plains.

Half a mile from the station, we come upon a dying horse, which the driver says had belonged to one of those soldiers who had gone before us. The beast is ripped through the belly; but whether he has been gored by a buffalo horn or slit open with a knife, we cannot decide as we roll swiftly by. Saddle and trapping have been taken away; but there is nothing to tell by whom, or for what end.

With fingers laced on our revolvers, we keep a keen eye upon objects, both far and near. At Chalk Bluff we find Kelly and Walden, the two stockmen, horribly scared. Kelly, an Irish lad, makes a wry face and a joke about the dirty vermin, who have just been here; but Walden, a Yankee, who has been through the war, is painfully white and grave. They believe these Cheyennes mean mischief. We give the brave lads a little cognac, wring their hands, and bid them be of good cheer, as we rattle off in the waggon.

(I am sorry to say, that three weeks afterwards these men were murdered by the Cheyennes. The Indians came to the hut, and, as usual, asked for food and tobacco. Kelly put their dinners on the table, which they instantly devoured. I cannot say how the poor men came to be so careless as they must have been, when the Cheyennes, catching them off their guard, lanced Kelly through the heart, and shot Walden in the bowels. Kelly fell dead, and Walden only lived a few hours. A waggon came up, and a white man heard the story from his lips.)

The whole road is unarmed, unprotected; for the two forts, Ellsworth and Wallace, each with a couple of weak companies, stand at a distance from each other of two hundred and twenty miles. If they are able to defend themselves it is thought enough. Pond Creek lies a mile from Fort Wallace: a woman and her daughter, Mrs. and Miss Bartholomew, live here; and when a party of Cheyennes came into the station yesterday, eating it up, and threatening to burn it down, the woman sent a driver up to the fort, which contains a garrison of one hundred and fifty men, with two field-pieces, and begged for help; but Lieutenant Bates, the gentleman in command, replied to her cry of distress, that if she and her daughter need protection, they must seek it in the lines, as he cannot spare a man to defend the road along which we are guarding the imperial mail!

She is packing a few things in a handkerchief, and as we drive out of the yard, we see the two women start off for the military post.

From Big Timber station, a place where we find a few trees, most welcome to our sight, the red-skins have hardly gone, as we roll in; they have been here three days, a party of twenty-eight, with Little Blanket at their head; eating the fat bacon, sipping the hot coffee, and lording over the stockmen like kings over conquered slaves. The country, they said, is theirs, and everything brought into it is theirs. When about to go away, they counted these trees, fifty-one in number. "No cut down trees," they said, "we like them to stand there, in the creek." Pointing to a stack of hay, laid up for the mules, they added, with a grim and smiling humour, "Cut grass, — cut plenty grass, — make big fire;" and, as they rode away, the chief turned round, and said, "Fifteen days we come back; you gone, good; you not gone — ugh!" accompanying his threat with a horrible pantomime, expressive of lapping flames.

At Cheyenne Wells we have another domestic scene. Long before coming to this station, we heard from drivers and train-men of Jack Dunbar, the station-keeper, as a reckless Colorado devil, one of those heroes of Sand Creek who had sent a slug into the heart of White Antelope, when the aged red-skin had bared his breast and called on the troops to fire.

We hoped to find one man, at least, unscared by this Indian raid along our line; but on our wheeling into his yard, we see that everything is wrong, for Dunbar has a wife at Cheyenne Wells, and his own share in the exploit of Sand Creek being well known to the Indians, he is fearful that the first sharp blow of the coming war may fall upon her head. A glance at the way-bill tells him that the stage is full, that passengers who have paid their hundreds of dollars have been left behind for want of room; but then, as he says, it is a question of life and death, — of a woman's life and death, — and he comes to us, cap in hand, with a prayer that we will carry on his wife into a place of safety. For himself, he is willing to stand by his stock, defending himself and his stable to the last; but the poor woman cannot fight, and in case of his own death, before he should have time to kill her, her fate would be revolting, far beyond the power of an English imagination to conceive.

What can we do, but offer to comply? A fresh disposal of the mail-bags; a new twist of our limbs; and a hole is made in the vehicle, into which the hero's wife inserts her slim and plastic body. A pillow thrust behind her head, protects her from many a bump and blow; but when we lift her, thirty hours later, from the waggon, it is hard to say whether she will live or die.

In the night, we rougher fellows get a little rest and relief by climbing to the box, breathing the cold air, and occasionally curling up our legs in the boot. It is only the fiery day that kills.

As the sun works westward towards his setting, the air grows cooler to the skin, softer in the lungs; and a spring of life comes back as it were into the veins. Our pulses quicken, our chests dilate, our limbs put out new strength. The weird and pensive solitude of the prairie grows into our souls as the stars peep out; and when the crescent moon lifts up her head from the horizon, bathing the vast ocean of rolling grass in her tender light, we feel in the beauty and majesty of Nature such a sovereign balm, that unless the scalping-knife were in his hand, we could salute either a Cheyenne or a Sioux as a man and a brother.

CHAPTER IX.

Red Communities.

BETWEEN the great lakes and the Gulf of Mexico, there may be two hundred tribes and tribelets of these red men: Creeks, Dakotas, Mohicans, Cheyennes, Pawnees, Shoshonees, Cherokees, Sioux, Comanches, and their fellows, more or less distinct in genius and in shape: men who once roamed over these hills and valleys, danced in their war-paint, hunted the elk and the bison, and left their long and liquid names to many American rivers and American states.

What to do with these forest people has been the thought of colonist and ruler from those early days when the first Saxon came into the land. At times, perhaps, an adventurer here and there has plied them too freely with the carbine and the cruse; but his better nature and his higher principle have brought him to regret this use of powder and whisky, the destroying angels of civilisation; and from the days of Penn, at least, the red man's right in the country has been commonly assumed by writers, and his claim to compensation for his lost hunting-ground has been recognised by the laws.

This policy of paying money for the land taken by the white men from the red was the more just and noble, as Indians, like the Senecas and the

Walla-Wallahs, have no clear sense of what is meant by rights in the soil. The soil? They know no soil. A Seneca comprehended his right to fish in the Hudson river; a Walla-Wallah understood his right to hunt bison in the plains at the feet of the Blue Mountains; but as a thing to plough and plant, to dig wells into, to build houses upon, the soil was no more to them than the sea and the sky are to us. A right to go over it they claimed; but to own it, and preserve it against the intrusion of all other men, is a claim which the red men have never made, and which, if they should learn to make it, could never be allowed by civilised men. No hunting tribe has any such right; perhaps no hunting tribe *can* have any such right; for, in strict political philosophy, the only exclusive right which any man can acquire in land, the gift of nature, is that which he creates for himself by what he puts into it by way of labour and investment alike for his own and for the common good. Now, a slayer of game does nothing for the land over which he roams; he clears no forest, he drains no marsh, he embanks no river, he plants no tree, he cultivates no garden, he builds no city; what he finds at his birth he leaves at his death; and no more property would, under such conditions, accrue to him in the soil than in the air. But, in dealing with such tribes as the Sioux and the Delawares, is it wise to be always bringing our political logic to the front? A law which the strong has to enforce, and which weighs upon the weak, may be tempered with mercy, even when it cannot be generally set aside. A little love, say the philanthropists, may go a long way. The land is here; we come and seize it; gaining for ourselves a possession of untold wealth, while driving the hunter from rivers and forests which before our coming had yielded his family the means of life. Ours is the profit, his the loss. Our wants can hardly be the measure of our rights; and if the Walla-Wallah has few rights in the soil, the stranger who displaces him has, in the first instance, none at all, beyond that vague common right which every human being may be supposed to possess in the earth on which he is born. A compromise, then, would appear to these reasoners to offer the only 'sound issue out of such conflicting claims; and an Englishman, jealous — for family reasons — of everything done by his brethren in the United States, may feel proud that, as between Yengees and Indians, the strong have dealt favourably with the weak.

Washington laid down a rule for paying to each tribe driven back from the sea by settlers a rental for their lands; arrangements for that purpose being made between a government agent and a recognised chief; and these payments to the Apalachian and Algonquin tribes and tribelets, have ever since that day been made by the United States government with unfailing good faith.

But a legal discharge of this trade obligation was far from being enough to satisfy conscientious men, who felt that in coming upon the Indian plain and forest they were driving a race of hunters from their fields, and cutting away from them the means by which they lived. Could nothing else be done for the red man? These white men saw that the past was past. A tribe of hunters, eating the flesh of antelope and buffalo, could not dwell in a province of farms and pastures. The last arrow had been shot when the homestead rose; it was only a question of years until the bow must be broken and the archer pushed aside. A hunter needs for his subsistence an area wide enough to feed thousands of men who can make their living by the plough and the spade. In a planet crowded like ours, no room can be found to grow the hunter's food; for the beaver which he traps, the elk which he runs down, the bison which he slays, will only breed in a country that is seldom disturbed by man. The smoke of a homestead drives away buffalo and deer. Even a pastoral tribe can find room enough only in the wilds of Asia and Africa, where the feuds between tent and city burn with consuming heat; yet a people living by pasturage, driving their flocks before them in search of herbage, require very little ground for their sustenance compared against a people living by the chase. What then? Must the red man perish from the earth? Should he die to let the white man live upon his land? Thousands of voices cried out against such sentence; at least until the white man, who had brought his law upon the scene, could say that every effort to save the Indian had been made, and that every experiment had failed.

Then came the question (only to be laid at rest by trial), whether the Seneca, the Delaware, the Oneida, and the Chippewa, could be trained in the arts of life; could be persuaded to lodge in framehouses, to live in one place, to plant corn and fruittrees, to wear trousers and shoes, to send their little ones to school? A number of pious persons, full of zeal for the red race, though lacking true knowledge of the course through which Nature works, put themselves to much cost and trouble in trying these experiments. These reformers had a strong belief in their power of doing things, so to say, by steam — of growing habits of life under glass, and of grafting civilisation with the knife. They fell to their work with unflinching spirit. Lands were given up to the red-skins; teachers were provided for them; schools, chapels, saw-mills, houses, were built for them; all the appliances of farming — ploughs and flails, corn-seed and fruit-trees, horses and oxen, poultry and pigs — were furnished, more or less freely, from the white man's stores. A true history of these trials would be that of a great endeavour, an almost uniform failure; fresh proof that Nature will not suffer her laws to be broken, her order contravened, and her grades disturbed.

A tribe of Senecas was placed upon the Alleghany river in a fine location; a tribe of Oneidas settled on a reservation, in the centre of New York, called Oneida Creek. Care and money were lavished on these remnants of red nations; farms were cleared, houses built for them; but they would not labour with their hands to any purpose; not with the caution, the continuity, needful to success in growing grain and stock. A good harvest made them lazy and improvident; a bad harvest thinned them by starvation and disease. One or two families, in whom there was a tinge of white blood, made pretty fair settlers; the rest only lived on the land so long as they could sell the timber and the game. As wood grew scarce, and game disappeared, they began to sell the land; at first to appointed agents; and to move away into the wild country of Green Bay. Most of the tribe have now left Oneida; — with the exception, perhaps, of the Walkers, all will quit their ancient Creek in time. Bill Beechtree, one of the remnants, cut me some hickory sticks, and showed me some bows and arrows which he makes for sale. He can do and will do nothing else. Though he never drew bow against an enemy in his life, and has a very nice voice for a psalm-tune, he considers any other occupation than cutting sticks and barbing arrows unworthy of the son of a brave.

The Delawares whom we saw near Leavenworth, the Pottawottamies whom we found at St. Mary's Mission, are in some respects better off than the Oneidas, being settled in the midst of friendly whites, among whom they continue to live, but only in a declining state. Both these tribes have engaged in farming and in raising stock. The Delawares rank among the noblest nations of the red men; they have finer forms, cleaner habits, quicker senses, than the Cheyennes and the Pawnees. A fragment of this people may be saved, by ultimate amalgamation with the surrounding whites, who feel less antipathy for them than for Sioux and Utes. The Pottawottamies have been lucky in attracting towards their settlement in Kansas the wise attentions of a Catholic bishop. At St. Mary's Mission, half-a-dozen priests have founded schools and chapels, taught the people religion, and trained them to habits of domestic life. Two thousand children are receiving lessons from these priests. The sheds are better built, the stock better tended, and the land better tilled, at St. Mary's than they are in the reservation of any Indian tribe that I have seen — except one.

At Wyandotte, on the Missouri river, some Shawnee families have been placed; and here, if anywhere in the Red Land, the friends of civilisation may point the moral of their tale. Armstrong, their chief and their richest man, has English blood in his veins; indeed, many of these Shawnees can boast of the same high title to respect among their tribe. They farm, they raise stock, they sell dry goods; some of them marry white girls, more give their daughters to whites; and a few among them aspire to the mysteries of banking and lending money. A special Act endows these Shawnees with the rank of citizens of Kansas, in which capacity they serve on juries and vote for members of Congress.

But the Shawnees of Wyandotte, being a people mixed in blood, can hardly be used as set-off against a score of undoubted failures.

CHAPTER X.

The Indian Question.

Now, the blame arising from these failures to found any large red settlement in the old countries once owned by Iroquois and Algonquin has been constantly charged against the red man. Is this charge a just one? Is it the Delaware's fault that he cannot pass in one generation from the state of a hunter into that of a husbandman? If a man should have his lodge built with a green shoot instead of with a strong tree, whose fault would it be when the lodge came down in a storm?

Everyone who has read the annals of our race — a page of nature, with its counterfoil in the history of everything having life — is aware that in our progress from the savage to the civilised state, man has had to pass through three grand stages, corresponding, as it were, to his childhood, to his youth, and to his manhood. In the first stage of his career, he is a hunter, living mainly by the chase; in the second stage, he is a herdsman, living mainly by the pasturage of goats and sheep, of camels and kine; in the third stage, he is a husbandman, living mainly by his cultivation of corn and maize, of fruits and herbs. These three conditions of human life may be considered as finding their purest types in such races as the Iroquois, the Arabian, and the Gothic, in their present stage;

but each condition is, in itself and for itself, an affair of development and not of race. The Arab, who is now a shepherd, was once a hunter; the Saxon, who is now a cultivator of the soil, was first a hunter, then a herdsman, before he became a husbandman. Man's progress from stage to stage is continuous in its course, obeying the laws of physical and moral change. It is slow; it is uniform; it is silent; it is unseen. In one word, it is growth.

No one can step at his ease from the first stage of human existence into the second; still less can he step from the first stage into the third. All growth is a work of time, depending on forces which are often beyond the control of art; work to be helped perhaps, not to be hurried, by men. As in the training of a vine, in the rearing of a child, a wise waiting upon nature seems our only course.

These three stages in our progress upward are strongly marked; the interval dividing an Iroquois from an Arab being as wide as that which separates an Arab from a Saxon.

The hunter's habits are those of a beast of prey. His teeth are set against everything having life; every beast on the earth, every bird in the air, being an enemy against which his club will be raised and his arrow will be drawn. On passing into the stage of a herdsman, he becomes used to the society of horses, dogs, and camels, animals of a tender breed; he finds himself charged with the care of sheep and goats, of cattle and fowls, creatures which he must pity and tend, bearing with their humours under penalty of their loss. If he would feed upon their milk and eggs, if he would clothe himself in their wools and skins, he must study their wants, and care for them with a parent's eye. It will become his business to serve and guard them; to seek out herbage and water for them; to consider their times and seasons; to prepare for them a shelter from the heats of noon and the frosts of night. Thus, a man's relation to the lower world of life must undergo a change. Where, in his savage state, he sharpened his knife against every living thing, he has now to become a student of nature, a nursing father to an ever-increasing family of beasts and birds.

Such cares as occupy all pastoral tribes — the Arab in his tent, the Caffir in his kraal, the Kirghis in his hut — are utterly unknown to the Seneca, the Shoshonee, and the Ute; the softer manners which result from the paternal relation of men to domestic animals having no existence in any hunting tribe. To advance from the stage of a Seneca into that of an Arab, is a march requiring many years, perhaps many generations, to accomplish; and even when that stage of pastoral existence shall have been gained, with all its changes of habit and of thought, the hunter will be only half-way on his path towards the position occupied by a grain-growing Saxon. After the second stage of this journey has been accomplished by the red man, those who have visited Nahr Debab in Syria, and watched the trials there being made by the Turks in settling the Ferdoon Arabs on the soil, will feel inclined to wait for any further results of his effort in a very calm and dispassionate frame of mind.

The Cheyenne is a wild man of the woods, whom neither cold nor hunger is strong enough to goad into working for himself, his children, and his squaws. How should it? A man may die of frost and snow, and even for lack of food, without bringing dishonour upon his tribe; but to labour with his hands is, in his simple belief, a positive disgrace. A warrior must not soil his palm with labour, seeing that his only duties in the world are to hunt and fight. If maize must be planted, if roots must be dug, if fires must be lit, if water must be carried, where is the squaw? Not much work is ever done in a Cheyenne lodge; but whether it be much or little, the man will take no part of the trouble upon himself. To kill his enemy and to catch his prey — that, in a line, is the Cheyenne's whole duty of man. Starvation itself will not drive him into treating industry as a duty; the neglect of which, even in another, is never, in his eyes, an offence. In some of the western tribes, where game is running scarce and the beavers evade the trap, the squaws and little ones throw a handful of grain into the soil; but the hunters give no heed to their work; and if, on their return to the spot, later in the year, the men find that their squaws have omitted to sow the maize, the idea of anybody working and waiting for a crop to grow is so foreign to their Indian taste, that they sit down and laugh at the neglect as a passing jest. If the tribe runs short of food, the hunter's remedy is to march against his neighbour, and by means of his bow and his tomahawk, to create a fresh balance between the mouths to be fed and the quantity of buffalo and elk which may be found to feed them. This rude remedy for want is his only art. Any thought of making the two ends of his account meet by setting up beehives and multiplying herds, would never present itself unbrought to his simple mind. His fathers having always been hunters, the only resource of his tribe, when their food runs short, is the original one of breaking through every obstacle to a fresh supply with his club.

Can we marvel, then, that when the Senecas were placed upon such land as the Alleghany reservation, in a bountiful and fruitful country, rich in white pines, and in other valuable trees, they should have done little or nothing in the way of planting and sowing; that they should have sold their timber to the whites; that they should have rented their saw-mills and ferries to the whites; that they should have let out their rafting yards and landing-places to the whites; in short, that they should have starved on a few dollars derived from rent, while the more eager and industrious Yankee, placed in the same location, would have coined the real riches of the country into solid gold? Like his Arab brother at Nahr Dehab, the Seneca on the Alleghany could not defile his hands with work, the business, not of warriors, but of squaws.

It is only fair, then, to remember, that the failure of so many attempts to convert the hunter into a husbandman at a single step was due to great laws of nature, not to the perversity of man. The chasm could not be bridged; but your eager and well-meaning friends of the red race, having no science to guide them, had to work this truth for themselves out of vague ideas into visible facts. In their ignorance of the general laws of growth, they saw their very sympathies and generosities changed into destroying powers; for the Indians who gave up their lands to the white men, receiving rentals or annuities in return for them, had to abandon their old habits of life without being able to enter on any new employments. And what was the end of this change for them? Hanging about the skirts of towns, they ate and drank, rioted and smoked, themselves into premature old age. Of a hundred millions of dollars which have been paid to the red man, it is said that fifty millions at least have been spent in grog-shops and in houses of evil name. The misery is, that in their savage state the red men have to live in the light of a high civilisation. The ferns which grow in their native forests would not more surely perish if they were suddenly planted out in the open sun.

The same hasty desire to bring the red savage into close relation with white civilisation affects the policy pursued by government agents in these Plains. In the American part of Red India failure of justice is the rule; in the Canadian part of Red India failure of justice is extremely rare; and the reason is this, the trappers and traders living beyond the Canadian frontier deal with robbery and murder with a promptness and simplicity unknown to American judges. My friend, Jem Baker, a sturdy old trapper, who resides with his squaws and papooses on Clear Creek, near Denver, put the whole case into a few words. "You see, colonel," says Jem, to whom every gentleman is a colonel, "the difference is this: if a Sioux kills a white man near Fort Ellice, you English say, 'Bring him in, dead or living, here's two hundred dollars;'. and when the Indians have brought him in, you say again, 'Try him for his life; if he is guilty, hang him on the nearest tree.' All is done in a day, and the Indians have his blood upon themselves. But, if a Sioux kills a white man near Fort Laramie, we Americans say, 'Bring him in with care, along with all the witnesses of his crime;' and when the Indians have brought him in, we say again, 'He must have a fair trial for his life; he must be committed by a justice and sent before a judge, he must have a good counsel to speak up for him, and a jury to try him who know nothing about his crime.' So most times he gets off, has a present from some lady perhaps, and goes back to his nation a big chief."

I have heard the details of cases in which Indian assassins, taken all but red-handed, have been sent to Washington for trial, three thousand miles away from the scenes and witnesses of their crimes; who, on being acquitted from the lack of such evidence as complicated legal methods require, have come back into these prairies, bearing on their arms and necks gifts of philanthropic ladies, and taking instant rank as leaders in their tribes. A simpler and swifter form of trial is needed on these Plains — on penalty of such irregular acts of popular vengeance as the battle of Sand Creek.

The truth is, the eastern cities have always

shirked the Indian question; fearing to face it boldly, hoping it would drop out of light and vex their spirits no more. "We push our way," said Secretary Seward to me, condolingly; "ninety years ago, my grandfather had the same sort of trouble with Indians, only sixty miles from New York, that you have now been suffering six hundred miles beyond St. Louis." I am often surprised by the splendid confidence which Americans express in their power of living down everything which they find unpleasant; but I am not convinced that this policy of pushing the red man off this continent is the only method of procedure.

If policy compels this people to make a new road from St. Louis to San Francisco, policy suggests that the road should be made safe. Thus much will be admitted in Boston as well as in Denver. But how is a path through the buffalo-runs to be made safe? By the white men going out every spring to beg a treaty of peace from Roman Nose and Spotted Dog, paying for it with baby talk, blankets, firearms, powder, and whisky? That is the present method of proceeding, and no one, except the agents, finds it much of a success. My own impression is, that such a method can have only one result, to deceive the red man into an utterly false impression of the white man's weakness. These Cheyennes actually believe that they are stronger, braver, and more numerous than the Americans. If one of these fellows, who may have been at St. Louis, reports to his tribe that the white men of the sunrise are many beyond counting, like the flowers on the prairie, they say that he has been seized by a bad spirit, and made into a speaker of lies. Thus, they hold the white men in contempt.

If these new roads are to be kept open, and blood is to be spared, this position of the white and red man should be reversed, and the order of things in this country made to correspond with the actual facts. The Indians must be driven into sueing for treaties of peace. If you admit their right to the land, buy it from them. When they come to you for peace, let them have it on generous terms, and then compel them to observe it with religious faith. A little severity may be necessary in the outset; for the Cheyenne has never yet felt the white man's power; but a policy, at once clear, clement and firm, would soon become intelligible to these sons of the prairie. If the policy of leaving things alone, and letting the trader, emigrant, and traveller, push their way through these deserts, is continued, the Americans will never cease to have trouble on their Indian frontiers.

CHAPTER XI.

City of the Plains.

At the head of these rolling prairies stands Denver, City of the Plains.

A few months ago, (time runs swiftly in these western towns; two years take you back to the middle ages, and a settler of five years' standing is a patriarch) Denver was a wifeless city.

"I tell you, sir," exclaimed a fellow-lodger in the wooden shanty known to emigrant and miner as the Planter's House, "five years ago, when I first came down from the gulches into Denver, I would have given a ten-dollar piece to have seen the skirt of a servant-girl a mile off."

This fellow was sitting at a lady's feet; a lady of middle age and fading charms; to whom, an hour or so afterwards, I said, "Pray, madam, is the gentleman who would have given the ten-dollar piece to see the skirt of a girl's petticoat, your husband?"

"Why do you ask, sir?"

Having had no particular reason for my query, I replied, with a bow, "Well, madam, I was rather hoping that so good a lover had met with a bright reward."

"No," she answered with a smile, "I am not his wife; though I might be to-morrow if I would. He has just buried one lady, and he wants to try on with a second."

On alighting at the Planter's House I had noticed, swinging near the door, a little sign, on which these words were painted —

"Madame Mortimer,
"Clairvoyant Physician."

In the shop-windows of Main Street I had seen a hand-bill, which appeared, from its ragged look, to have done service in some other house, of dirty habits, announcing that the celebrated Madame Mortimer had arrived in Denver, and might be consulted daily (no address being given) on what I may, perhaps, be allowed to call diseases of the heart. Her room in the hotel stood next in the corridor to mine, and as a large panel over her door (door discreetly locked) leading from my room into hers was open, I could at any time of the last three or four nights and days have made her personal acquaintance by simply standing on tip-toe and looking through. Strange to say, I have not thought of arming myself against the wiles of my neighbour, even by a cursory inspection of her camp; and when, I spoke just now to the faded woman in the parlour, I was utterly unaware that she was the celebrated Madame Mortimer, who could tell everybody's fortune — show every man a portrait of his future wife, every woman a picture of her future husband — for the low charge of two dollars per head!

Poor sorceress! there is not much poetic charm

in her; not a tradition of the art, the grace, and suppleness of spirit which made the genuine witch. This afternoon, in passing my door in the lobby, with the adoring lover at her heels, she saw me looking on the ground for something. It was only a match, which I had dropped while drawing on the wall for a light.

"You have lost something?"

"Madam, it is only a match; can you make me a new one?" said I, looking from her face to that of the miner.

"We do not make matches in Denver," she replied, in the saddest spirit.

"Surely they cannot help making them wherever you are," I said with a bow.

She looked quite blank, though the lover began to chuckle. "How?" she asked, still simpering.

"How! by gift and grace of heaven, where all matches are made."

At last she smiled. "Ha! thank you, sir; I like that, and will keep it;" on which she and the lover slipt away into the parlour; and I lit my cigar with a fusee. Yet this poor sorceress is a feature in the City of the Plains; and I am told that, while the bloom of her coming was fresh among these mining men, the curiosity about her was keen, the flow of dollars into her pocket steady. But the charm appears to be nearly spent; the landlord, properly protected by a wife, and not being of a romantic turn, is said to be dunning her for bills; and she is consequently being driven by adverse fates to trifle with the affections on her own account. Her life in this city of rakes and gamblers must have been a very hard one; the nearest town is six hundred miles away; the price of a seat in the stage is about two hundred dollars. Poor artist in fate — the stars appear to be very hard on her just now!

(*Note.* On my return from Salt Lake City to Denver. I found that her little sign had been removed from the house-front, and I began to fear that she had been driven off by adverse angels to either Leavenworth or Omaha; but in skipping upstairs to my room I met the poor creature on the landing-stage, and made her my politest bow. From a friend in the house I learned that she had retired from her profession into domestic life; but only, I am grieved to add, with what, in this City of the Plains, is described as the brevet rank of lady and wife.)

The men of Denver, even those of the higher classes, though they have many strong qualities — bravery, perseverance, generosity, enterprise, endurance — heroic qualities of the old Norse gods, — are also, not unlike the old Norse gods, exceedingly frail in morals; and where you see the tone of society weak, you may always expect to find aversion to marriage, both as a sentiment and as an institution, somewhat strong. Men who have lived alone, away from the influence of mothers and sisters, have generally but a faint belief in the personal virtue and fidelity of women; and apart from this lack of belief in woman, which ought to be a true religion in the heart of every man, the desire for a fixed connexion and a settled home will hardly ever spring up. Men may like the society of women, and yet not care to encumber themselves for life. The worst of men expect, when they marry, to obtain the best of wives; but the best of women do not quit New England and Pennsylvania for Colorado. Hence it is a saying in Denver, — a saying confirmed by practice, — that in these western cities, though few of the miners have wives, you will not find many among them who can be truly described as marrying men.

On any terms short of marriage these lusty fellows may be caught by a female snare. They take very freely to the charms of negresses and squaws. One of the richest men of this city, whose name I forbear to give, has just gone up into the mountains with a couple of Cheyenne wives. Your young Norse gods are nervously afraid of entering into a Christian church.

Denver is a city of four thousand people; with ten or twelve streets laid out; with two hotels, a bank, a theatre, half-a-dozen chapels, fifty gambling-houses, and a hundred grog-shops. As you wander about these hot and dirty streets, you seem to be walking in a city of demons.

Every fifth house appears to be a bar, a whisky-shop, a lager-beer saloon; every tenth house appears to be either a brothel or a gaming-house; very often both in one. In these horrible dens a man's life is of no more worth than a dog's. Until a couple of years ago, when a change for the better began, it was quite usual for honest folks to be awakened from their sleep by the noise of exploding guns; and when daylight came to find that a dead body had been tossed from a window into the street. No inquiry was ever made into the cause of death. Decent people merely said, "Well, there is one sinner less in Denver, and may his murderer meet his match to-morrow!"

Thanks to William Gilpin, founder of Colorado, and governor elect, aided by a Vigilance Committee; thanks also to the wholesome dread which unruly spirits have conceived of the quick eye and resolute hand of Sheriff Wilson; thanks, more than all, to the presence of a few American and English ladies in the streets of Denver, the manners of this mining pandemonium have begun to change. English women who have been here two or three years assure me it is greatly altered. Of course, Gilpin is opposed — in theory, at least — to all such jurisdiction as that exercised by the Vigilance Committee; but for the moment, the society of this city is unsettled, justice is blind and lame, while violence is alert and strong; and the Vigilance Committee, a secret irresponsible board, acting above all law, especially in the matter of life and death, has to keep things going by means of the revolver and the rope. No one knows by name the members of this stern tribunal; every rich, every active, man in the place is thought to be of it; and you may hear, in confidential whispers, the names of persons who are supposed to be its leaders, ministers, and executioners. The association is secret, its agents are many, and nothing, I am told, escapes the knowledge, hardly anything escapes the action, of this dread, irresponsible court. A man disappears from the town:—it is an offence to inquire about him; you see men shrug their shoulders; perhaps you hear the mysterious words — "Gone up." Gone up, in the slang of Denver, means gone up a tree — that is to say, a cotton-tree — by which is meant a particular cotton-tree growing on the town creek. In plain English, the man is said to have been *hung*. This secret committee holds its sittings in the night, and the time for its executions is in the silent hours between twelve and two, when honest people should be all asleep in their beds. Sometimes, when the storekeepers open their doors in Main Street, they find a corpse dangling on a branch; but commonly the body is cut down before dawn, removed to a suburb, where it is thrown into a hole like that of a dead dog. In most cases, the place of burial is kept a secret from the people, so that no legal evidence of death can be found.

Swearing, fighting, drinking, like the old Norse gods, a few thousand men, for the most part wifeless and childless, are engaged, in these upper parts of the Prairie, in founding an empire. The expression is William Gilpin's pet phrase; but the congregation of young Norse gods who drink, and swear, and fight along these roads, are comically unaware of the glorious work in which they are engaged.

"Well, sir," said to me, one day, a burly stranger, all boots and beard, with a merry mouth and audacious eye; "well, what do you think of our Western boys?"

Remembering Gilpin, and wishing to be safe and complimentary, I replied, "You are making an empire." "Eh?" he asked, not understanding me, and fancying I was laughing in my sleeve — a liberty which your Western boy dislikes — he brought his hand, instinctively, a little nearer to his bowie-knife. "You are making an empire?" I put in once again, but by way of inquiry this time, so as to guard against giving offence and receiving a stab.

"I don't know about that," said he, relaxing his grim expression, and moving his hand from his belt: "but I am making money."

Gilpin, I daresay, would have laughed, and said it was all the same.

William Gilpin is perhaps the most noticeable man on the Plains, just as Brigham Young is the most noticeable in the Salt Lake Valley; and it would hardly be a figure of speech to say that his office in Denver (a small room in the Planter's House, which serves him for a bed-room, for a library, for a hall of audience, for a workshop, and the upper ten thousand of Colorado, generally, for a spittoon,) is the high school of politics for the gold regions and the mountain districts. By birth, Gilpin is a Pennsylvanian; by nature and habit, a state founder. Descending from one of the best Quaker families of his state, (his ancestor was the Gilpin who came out with Penn and Logan,) taught by history the need of that large and graceful tolerance of religious sentiment which Penn displayed in the court of Charles the Second, which the Friends have put into practice on the Susquehannah, and armed by nature with abundant gifts of genius, —

patience, insight, eloquence, enthusiasm, — he has played, and he is now playing, a singular and dramatic part in this western country. He describes himself to me as in sympathy a Quaker-Catholic: that is to say, as a man who embraces in his single person the extremes of religious thought — the feeling of personality with the dogma of authority — the laxest forms of liberty with the sternest canons of order; an unusual blending of sentiments and sympathies, one not made in a day, not springing from an individual whimsy, but the result of much history, of a long family tradition; and nowhere, perhaps, to be found in this generation except on the frontier-land which unites Quaker Pennsylvania with Catholic Delaware. Gilpin abounds in apparent contradictions. A Quaker, he is also a soldier — a West Pointer — and of singular distinction in his craft. He bore a prominent part in the Mexican war; was the youngest man in the army who attained the rank of lieutenant-colonel; and but for his resignation, on moving out west, would have been the superior officer of Grant and Sherman. It is a happy circumstance for him that no call of duty made it necessary for him to hold prominent command against any section of his countrymen during the civil war. Gilpin's work is in another field, in the Great West, of which he is the champion and the idol; and which he has given his mind to explore, to advertise, to settle, and to subdue.

Under this man's sway, the city is changed, and is changing fast; yet, if I may believe the witnesses, the advent of a dozen English and American ladies,

8*

who came out with their husbands, has done far more for Denver than the genius and the eloquence of William Gilpin. A lady is a power in this country. From the day when a silk dress and a lace shawl were seen in Main Street, that thoroughfare became passably clean and quiet; oaths were less frequently heard; knives were less frequently drawn; pistols were less frequently fired. None of these things have ceased; far, very far, is Denver yet from peace; but the young Norse gods have begun to feel rather ashamed of swearing in a lady's presence, and of drawing their knives before a lady's face.

Slowly, but safely, the improvement has been brought about. At first, the ladies had a very bad time, as their idiom runs. They feared to associate with each other; every woman suspected her neighbour of being little better than she should be. Things are safer now; and I can testify, from experience, that Denver has a very charming, though a very limited, society of the better sex.

CHAPTER XII.

Prairie Justice.

The chief executive officer of this city is Robert Wilson, sheriff, auctioneer, and justice of the peace; though he would hardly be recognised in Colorado under such a description. As Quintus Horatius Flaccus, poet and good-fellow, is only known as Horace, so Robert Wilson, sheriff and auctioneer, is only known as Bob, in polite society as Bob Wilson. The Sheriff, who is said, like our Judge Popham of immortal memory, to have been a gambler, if nothing worse, in his wild youth, is still a young-looking man of forty or forty-two; a square, strong-chested fellow, low in stature, with a head like the Olympian Jove's. The stories told in the Prairies of this man's daring make the blood freeze, the flesh creep, and the pulse gallop. To-day he came and sat with me for hours, talking of the city and the territory in which his fortunes are all bound up. One of his tales was that of his capture of three horse-stealers.

According to the code in fashion here in Denver, murder is a comparatively slight offence. Until two or three years ago, assassination — incidental, not deliberate assassination — was a crime of every day. At the door of some gambling-house — and every tenth house in Main Street was a gambling-house, openly kept, with the stimulants of drinking, singing, and much worse — it was a common thing to find a dead man in the streets each day-break. A fight had taken place over the roulette-table; pistols had been drawn; and the fellow who was slowest with his weapon had gone down. No one thought of searching into the affray. A ruffian had been shot, and the city considered itself free of so much waste. Human life is here of no account; and what man likes to bring down upon himself the vengeance of a horde of reckless devils by seeking too particularly into the cause of a fellow's death?

A lady, whom I met in Denver, wife of an ex-mayor of that city, told me that when she first came out into the West, four or five years ago, there were sixty persons lying in the little graveyard, excluding criminals, not one of whom had died a natural death. Exact enquiry told me this account was somewhat beyond the mark; but her statement showed the belief still current in the best houses; and, indeed, it was only a little beyond the truth. Men quarrel in the streets and fight, but no one dreams of going to the help of the weaker side. One night, when I was writing in my room, a pistol-shot exploded near my window, and, on looking out, I saw a man writhing on the ground. In a few moments he was carried off by his comrades; no one followed his assailant; and I heard next day, that the assassin was not in custody, and that no one knew for certain where he was. Opposite my window there is a well, at which two soldiers were drinking water late at night; an English gentleman, standing on the balcony of the Planter's House, heard one soldier say to the other, "Look, there is a cobbler, bang at him!" on which his comrade raised his piece and fired. Poor Crispin jumped up into his shop and shut the door; he had a near escape with life, for the ball had gone through the boarding of his house, and lodged itself in the opposite wall. Nothing was done to those two soldiers; and every one to whom I expressed my surprise at such negligence on the part of their commanding officers, marvelled at my surprise.

Unless a ruffian is known to have killed half-a-dozen people, and to have got, as it were, murder on the brain, he is almost safe from trouble in these western plains. A notorious murderer lived near Central City; it was known that he had shot six or seven men; but no one thought of interfering with him on account of his crimes until he was taken red-handed in the very act. Some persons fancied he was heartily sorry for what he had done, and he himself, when tossing off cocktails with his rough companions, used to say he was sick of shedding blood.

One day, on riding into Central City, he met a friend whom he invited to take a drink. The friend, not wishing to be seen any more in such bad company, declined the offer, on which the ruffian drew his pistol in the public street, in the open day, and saying, with a comic swagger of reluctance, "Good God, can I never come into town without killing some one?" shot his friend through the heart. Seized by the indignant crowd, the callous ruffian had a stern trial, a short shrift, and a midnight escape up the famous cotton-tree in the city ditch.

But with respect to theft, most of all the theft of horses, public opinion is far more strict than it is with respect to murder. Horse-stealing is always punished by death. Five good horses were one day missed from a corral in Denver; and on Wilson being consulted as to the probable thieves, the Sheriff's suspicions fell on three mining rowdies, gamblers and thieves, named Brownlee, Smith, and Carter, men who had recently come into the city from the mines and the mountain roads. As enquiry in the slums and grog-shops could not find these worthies, Wilson, feeling sure that they were the men he wanted, ordered his horse, and, after looking well at his revolver and bowie-knife, jumped into the saddle and turned towards the Platte road. The time was early spring, when the snow was melting and the water high. Coming to the river, he stript and crossed the rapids, holding his clothes and pistols above his head, and partly swimming his horse across the stream. Riding on all day, all night, he came upon the thieves on a lonely prairie, one hundred and fifty miles from Denver, and five miles from the nearest ranch. Carter and Smith were each leading a horse, in addition to the one he rode; Brownlee rode alone, bringing up the rear. It was early day when he came up with them, and, as they did not know him by sight, he entered into conversation, chiefly with Brownlee, passing himself off with the robbers as a broken miner going home to the States; and riding with them from eight o'clock until twelve, in the hope of meeting either the public stage, or some party of traders who could lend him help. But he looked in vain. At noon he saw that no assistance could be got that day, and feeling that he must do his perilous work alone, he suddenly changed his air and voice, and reining in his horse, said:—

"Gentlemen, we have gone far enough; we must turn back."

"Who the h—— are you?" shouted Brownlee, drawing his weapon.

"Bob Wilson," said the Sheriff, quietly; "come to fetch you back to Denver. You are accused of stealing three horses. Give up your arms, and you shall be fairly tried."

"You go to h——!" roared Brownlee, raising his pistol; but, before he could draw the trigger, a slug was in his brain, and he tumbled to the ground with the imprecation hot upon his lips. Smith and Carter, hearing the loud words behind them followed by the exploding pistol, turned round suddenly in their saddles and got ready to fire; but in the confusion Smith let drop his piece; and, in an eye-blink, Carter fell to the ground, dead as the dust upon which he lay. Smith, who had jumped down from his horse to get his pistol, now threw up his hands.

"Come here," cried Wilson, to the surviving thief; "hold my horse; if you stir a limb, I fire; you see I am not likely to miss my mark."

"You shoot very clean, sir," answered the trembling ruffian.

"Now, mind me," said the Sheriff; "I shall take you and these horses back to Denver; if you have stolen them, so much the worse for you; if not, you are all square; any way you shall have a fair trial."

Wilson then picked up the three pistols, all of them loaded and capped. "I hesitated for a moment," he said to me, in this part of his tale, "whether to draw the charges; on second thought I resolved to keep them as they were, as no one could tell what might happen." Tying the three pistols in a handkerchief, and carefully re-loading his own revolver, he then bade Smith get on one of the horses, to which he then made the fellow fast by ropes passed round his legs. Leaving the two dead men on the ground, and turning the horses loose to graze, Wilson led his captive along the road as far back as the ranch. A French settler, with an English wife, lived at this prairie ranch, and on Wilson stating who he was, and what his prisoner was more than suspected of being, the brave couple entered into his plans. After lashing Smith to a post, and telling the woman to shoot him dead if he struggled to get free (an order which her husband said she would certainly carry out, should the need for it arise), the two men rode back to the scene of execution, buried the two bodies, recovered the four horses, and brought away many articles from the dead men's pockets, which might serve to identify them in evidence. Returning to the ranch, they found the woman on guard, and Smith in despair. In their absence, Smith had used all his arts of appeal upon the woman; he had appealed to her pity, to her vanity, to her avarice. At length she had been forced to tell him that she would hear no more, that if he spoke again she would fire into his mouth. Then he grew white and silent. Next day brought the Sheriff and his prisoner to Denver, when Smith had a short shrift and a violent escape up the historical tree.

CHAPTER XIII.

Sierra Madre.

FROM Denver City up to Bridger's Pass, the highest point of the Sierra Madre (Mother Crest, or saw-line), over which trapper and trader have worn a track, the ascent is easy as to gradients, though it may be most uneasy in the matter of ruts, creeks, sand and stones. So far a traveller finds but little difference between the mountains and the prairies, which are also rolling uplands, rising between Leavenworth and Denver upwards of four thousand feet, the height of Snowdon above the sea. Yet Bridger's Pass is the water-parting of a great continent; the eastern slopes shedding their snow and rain towards the Atlantic Ocean, the western slopes towards the Pacific Ocean.

For ninety miles the road runs quietly north of Denver, along the base of a lower range of mountains known as the Black Hills, in search of an opening through the towering wall of rock and snow. At Stonewall, near Virginia Dale, it finds a gorge, or canyon, as the people call it, leading into a pretty woodland district, full of springs and streamlets, in which the trout are so abundant you may catch them in a creel. The scenery is not yet wild and grand, though it is picturesque, from the strange rock formation and the brilliance of its body colour. The moment you enter into the mountain land, you see why the Spaniards called it Colorado. The prevailing tint of rock, of soil, of tree (especially in the fall), is red.

Between Virginia Dale and Willow Springs, the country lying south of our track may be called beautiful. The road runs high, commanding a sweep of many valleys, bright with welcome foliage, therefore blessed with water; broken by cols and ridges, with long dark intervals of space between; the whole landscape crowned in the distance by the mighty and irregular range from Long's Peak to Pike's Peak. This is a true Swiss scene; the hills being clothed with pine, the summits capped with snow; a scene as striking in its natural features as the more famous view of the Oberland Alps from Berne.

At Laramie we lose this mountain picture. Low mounds of earth and sand, covered with the wild sage, peopled by prairie dogs, coyotes, and owls, shut out the snow-line from our sight.

Here and there along the track we pass the shoulder, we cross the summit, of a height which may be called a mountain (out of courtesy), such as Elk Mountain, the Medicine Bow Mountain, and the ridge of North Platte, before we descend upon Sage Creek and Pine Grove; but we see no peaks, we climb no alps; jog jog, — trot trot, — grind grind, — we rumble in the light waggon over stones, over grass, over sand, across creeks and water-ruts, with a uniform misery, day after night, night after day, that would murder any man outright, from sheer exhaustion of his animal spirits, were it not for the strong reaction caused by the ever-expected appearance of Ute, Cheyenne, and Sioux.

The life is hard at its best, intolerable at its average. Only twice in the night and day we are allowed to eat. The food is bad, the water worse, the cooking worst. Vegetables there are none. Milk, tea, butter, beef, mutton, are commonly wanting. Even the talismanic letters from New York are useless in these high and desolate Passes through the sage-fields. If there were food, it would be sold to us; but, as a rule, there is simply none at all. Hot dough, which they call cake, you may have, though you will find it hard to eat, impossible to digest — you who are not to the material and the method born, and who have been pampered and spoiled by the *chefs* in Pall Mall. No beer, no spirit, sometimes no salt, can be found. As a luxury, you may get dried elk and buffalo-flesh, seasoned with a dash of powder; and for these horrid dainties you are charged a dollar and a half, in some places two dollars per meal.

But if the life seems hard to us, who get through it in a dozen days and nights, what must it prove to the trapper, the teamster, the emigrant? Spite of its perils and privations, this mountain road is alive with trains of people going to and fro between the River and Salt Lake. Hundreds of men, thousands of oxen, mules, and horses, climb these desolate tracks; bearing with them, in light mountain waggons built for the purpose, the produce of eastern fields and cities, — green apples, dried corn, salt beef, flour, meal, potted fruits and meats, — as well as

tea, tobacco, coffee, rice, sugar, and a multitude of
dry goods, from caps and shoes to coffin-plates and
shrouds, — bearing them to the mining districts of
Colorado, Utah, Idaho, Montana, where such things
find a ready sale. The train-men march in bands
for safety, and a train from Leavenworth to Salt
Lake resembles in many ways the great caravan of
commerce on a Syrian road. A trader on the river,
— at Omaha, in Nebraska, — at Leavenworth, in
Kansas, — hears, or perhaps suspects, that some
article, such as tea, cotton, fruits, — it may be molasses, tanned leather, — is running short in the
mountains, and that in a few weeks a demand for it
is likely to spring up at high rates. Buying in a
good market, he takes the risk of being wrong in
his conjecture. With his one prime article of trade
he combines a dozen minor articles; say, with a huge
bulk of tea, a little cutlery, a little claret, a little
quinine and other drugs, store of blankets and
gauntlets, — perhaps a thousand pairs of top-boots.
He buys fifty or sixty light waggons, with a dozen
oxen to each waggon; engages a train boss, or captain, hires about a hundred men, packs up his goods,
and sends the caravan off into the plains. No actuary
in his senses would ensure the arrival of that train
in Denver, in Salt Lake, in Virginia city. The
journey is considered as an adventure. The men
who go with it must be excellent shots, thoroughly
well armed; but they are not expected to defend
their cargo against the Indians; and should the redskin plunderers show in force, the teamsters are
allowed to cut the traces, mount on the fleetest mules,

and fly to the nearest post or station, leaving their waggon, stock, and cargo, to be plundered as the Indians list. No man likes his poll to be scalped; and the teamster, with a wife and child, perhaps, lying in Omaha, in Leavenworth, loves to keep his hair untouched. Murder will happen in the best-conducted trains; but the bravest Western boy sets his life above a hundred chests of tea and a thousand sacks of flour.

Some of these trains haul passengers along the road at the rate of fifty dollars a-head for the journey — (in the stage it is two hundred and fifty) — the passenger finding himself in food, herding with the teamsters, and cooking his own meals.

The trip, when it is done at all, is made in about ninety days, from the River to Salt Lake; a journey of more than twelve hundred miles; with the city of Denver as a resting-place, six hundred miles from the starting-point and from the end. The average rate is fourteen or fifteen miles a-day; though some of the train-men will push through twenty miles on the plains.

Four or five hours in the middle of the day they rest to let the cattle graze, and to cook their food; at night-fall they encamp near to fresh water, if possible in the vicinity of a little wood. They corral the waggons; that is to say, they set them in the form of an ellipse, open only at one end, for safety; each waggon locked against its neighbour, overlapping it by a third of the length, like the scales on plate armour; this ellipse being the form of defence against Indian attack, which long experience in frontier warfare had proved to the old Mexican traders in these regions to be the most effective shield. When the waggons are corralled, and the oxen are turned loose to graze, the men begin to cut and break wood, the women and children (if there be any in the party) light the fires, fetch water from the spring or creek, boil the kettle, and bake the evening bread. Some of the young men, expert with the rifle, tramp across gully and creek in search of plover, prairie dog, and chicken; and on lucky days these hunters may chance to fall upon antelope and elk. Luck going with them, the evening closes with a feast. Others hunt for rattle-snakes, and kill them; also for stray coyotes and wolves, many of which, driven mad by hunger, infest the neighbourhood of a camp. I saw a huge grey wolf shot within two yards of a waggon, which had been lifted from the wheels and set on the ground, and in which lay a sleeping child. When supper is done, the oxen, having had their mouthful of bunch-grass, are driven for safety into the corral of waggons; otherwise the morning light would haply find them miles away in an Indian camp. A song, a story, perhaps a dance, winds up the weary day. In warm weather, train folks sleep in the waggons, to escape the rattle-snakes and wolves. When the snow is deep in the gulley, when the wind comes sweeping down the ice, a waggon on wheels is too cold for a bed, and the trainmen prefer a blanket on the ground, with a whisky-bottle for a pillow. Long before dawn they are up and about; yoking the cattle, hitching up the waggons, swallowing their morning meal. Sunrise finds them plodding on the road.

Sometimes the owner travels with his train; not often; for the boss can manage these unruly, drunken, quarrelling teamsters better than the actual owner of the cargo. If the rations should run short, if the whisky should turn out bad, if the waggons should break down, the boss can join chorus with the teamsters in swearing at his chief. A strong outburst of abuse is said to do the men much good; and as the owner does not hear it, he is none the worse. When the chief is present, every man in the train has a complaint to make; so that time is lost by the way, and a spirit of insubordination shows itself in the camp. When anything goes wrong — and every day, in such a country, something must go wrong — if the real master is not present, the boss can say, *he* cannot help it, they are all in one boat, and they must make the best of a bad job. In this way — grumbling, drinking, fighting — they get through the mountain-passes; to end their ninety days of stern privations by a week's debauchery, either in the secret slums of Salt Lake City, or in the solitude of some mountain ranch.

The owner travels in the mail, more swiftly, not more pleasantly, than his servants, and is ready in Denver, in Salt Lake, in Virginia City, to receive his waggons; when he may sell the whole train, tea, drugs, hosiery, waggons, oxen, in a lump or lumps.

The ranch-men are of two classes; (1), the enterprising class, who go out into the mountains —

much as eastern farmers go into the back-woods — to clear the ground, to grow a little corn, to feed a few sheep and kine; fighting the battle of life, on one side against reluctant nature, on the other side against hostile red-skins; living on bad food and bad water, in the hope of getting a first footing on the unoccupied soil, and laying the foundation of a fortune for their sons and grandsons; (2), the more reckless class, who build a log-hut by the roadside, in the highway of teamster and emigrant, with a view of selling whisky and cordials to the passers-by, and even to the tipsy Cheyenne and Sioux, making in a brief season a fortune for themselves. Both classes lead a life of much peril and privation. Even more than the teamster and the emigrant, the ranch-man bears his life in the palm of his hand; for every ruffian on the road who calls for drink, with a bowie-knife and a revolver in his belt, has the quick, quarrelsome spirit of the Western boy, and often wants whisky to drink when he has never a dollar in his pouch to pay for the delicious dram.

But the chief peril comes to the ranch-man in the shape of Indians; most of all, when a powerful tribe, like that of the Sioux, that of the Pawnees, sets out on the war-path. The red-skin loves whisky more than he loves either wife or child; in peace he will sell anything to obtain his darling poison; his papoose, his squaw, even his captive in war: but when a Sioux has put the red paint on his cheek, and slung the scalping-knife to his side, he no longer thinks of buying his dose of fire-water from the white man, he sweeps down upon the ranch, takes it by force, and with it, not unfrequently, the life of its vendor.

Yet the spirit of gain tempts the ranch-man to rebuild his burnt shed, to replenish his plundered store. If he lives through two or three seasons of successful trade in whisky and tobacco, he is rich. Paddy Blake, an Irishman, from Virginia city, keeps a ranch near the summit of Bridger's Pass, in a field which is the very model of desolation. He lives at Fort Laramie; by trade he is a sutler; but he finds it pay better to sell bad spirits to the teamsters at three dollars a bottle, and cake-tobacco for chewing at six dollars a pound, than to deal in decent stores among soldiers and civilians at the fort. A small log-hut contains his stock of poisons, which he vends to the passer-by, including Utes and Cheyennes, about four months in the year, while the roads are open and the snow is off the ground; taking buffalo and beaver skins from the red men, dollars and kind (the kind too often stolen) from the whites.

Along this mountain road, in every train, among the callous teamsters, among the raw emigrants, among the passing strangers, among the resident stockmen, there is one topic of conversation night and day, — the Indians. Every red man moves in this region with the scalping-knife in his hand. Spottiswood, one of the smart agents of the Overland mail, told me that he saw a white man taken by the Sioux from his waggon, and burnt to death on a pile of bacon. The antelope-hunter of Virginia

Dale was killed only a few weeks ago. Between Elk Mountain and Sulphur Springs a train was stopped by Cheyennes, and eighteen men, women, and children, were massacred and mutilated. Two young girls were carried off, and, after being much abused by the Indians, were sent into Fort Laramie, and exchanged for sacks of flour from the quartermaster's store.

Near the top of the first pass stands a lonely mail-station, called, by a pious and permissible fiction, Pine Grove; two stockmen occupy the log-hut; one of them, named Jesse Ewing, is the hero of a tale more striking than many a deed that has earned the Victoria Cross.

In the spring of this year a party of Sioux, then out on the war-path, came to Pine Grove, and by accident found Jesse there alone. As usual, they made free with what was not their own; ate up the bread and coffee, the dried elk, and the salt bacon; and having gorged their stomachs, they told Jesse to light a big fire, as they meant to roast him alive. Burning their captives is a common pastime with the Sioux; not their Pawnee enemies only, but the Swaps (as they call the Yengees) or Pale-faces also. Up to this time Jesse had contrived to keep his knife and his revolver hidden in his clothes, and neither of these weapons being seen, the Indians supposed that he was quite unarmed and at their mercy. At first, he refused to light a fire, knowing they would carry out their threat; and on their saying they would set their squaws to skin him if he did not swiftly obey their chief, he said he could not make a big fire unless he were allowed to fetch straw and faggots from the stable. The fact being obvious to the Sioux, he was told to go and fetch them, two of the Indians going out into the night to see him do it; one entering the stable with him, the second standing at the door on guard. Quick as thought, his knife was in the side of the red man near him; a second later a slug was in the brain of the one outside. The firing brought out all the yelping band; but Jesse, swift as an antelope, leaped into a creek, got under some trees and stones, in a place which he knew very well, and lay there under cover, still as the dead, while the Sioux, infuriated by their sudden loss, kept up for hours around his hiding-place their wild and horrible yep, yep. The night was intensely cold; he had no shoes; no coat: worse than all else, the snow began to fall, so that he could not stir without leaving traces of his feet along the ground. Happily for him, snow slobbers and numbs an Indian's feet as quickly as it chills a Yengee's. He could hear the Sioux crying out against the cold; after a few hours he found that his enemies were turning their faces eastward. Slowly, the noise of feet and voices bore away; the Indians taking the path towards Sage Creek; and when the air was a little still, Jesse stole from his covert, and ran for his life to the home-station at Sulphur Springs, where he arrived at daybreak, and obtained from his comrades of the road the welcome relief of food and fire.

This brave boy has come back to Pine Grove;

a fact which I mention with regret, since the Indians are again menacing the road; and if they come down in strength, Jesse will be marked in their score of vengeance as one of the first to fall.

CHAPTER XIV.

Bitter Creek.

The Camp of Peaks, composing the Sierra Madre, having their crown and centre in Fremont's Peak, three hundred feet above the height of Monte Rosa, shed from their snowy sides three water-lines; on the eastern side, towards the Mississippi and the Atlantic Ocean; on the western side, towards the Columbia river and the Pacific Ocean; on the southern side, towards the Colorado river and the Gulf of California. South-westward of this Peak rises the Wasatch chain, shutting out from these systems of rain-flow the depression known as the Valley of Utah and the Great Salt Lake. Between the two great mountain chains of the Sierra Madre and the Wasatch lies the Bitter Creek country, one of the most sterile spots on the surface of this earth.

This wild Sahara, measuring it from Sulphur Springs to Green river, is one hundred and thirty-five miles in width. It is a region of sand and stones, without a tree, without a shrub, without a spring of fresh water. Bones of elk and antelope, of horse and bullock, strew the ground. Here and there, more thickly than elsewhere, you come upon a human grave; each of which has a story known to the mountaineers. This stone is the memorial of five stock-men who were murdered by the Sioux.

Yon pole marks the resting-place of a young emigrant girl, who died on her way to the Promised Land. That tree is the gallows of a wretch, who was hung by his companions in a drunken brawl. The whole track is marked by skeletons and tragedies; and visible nature is in sternest harmony with the work of man. A little wild sage grows here and there, scattered in lonely bunches in the midst of a weak and stunted grass. The sun-flower all but disappears, attaining, where it grows at all, no more than the size of a common daisy. The hills are low, and of a dirty yellow tint. A fine white film of soda spots the landscape, here in broad fields, there in bright patches, which the unused eye mistakes for frost and snow. When the creek, which lends its bitter name to the valley, is full of water, as in early summer, while the ice is melting, the taste of that water, though nauseous, may be borne; but when the creek runs dry, in the later summer and the fall, it is utterly abominable to man and beast; rank poison, which inflames the bowels and corrupts the blood. Yet men must drink it, or they die of thirst; cattle must drink it, or they will die of thirst. The soil is very heavy, the road is very bad. A train can hardly cross this Bitter Creek country under a week, and many of the emigrant parties have to endure its stern privations ten or twelve days. Oxen cannot pull through the heavy sand, when from scanty food and poisonous drink their strength has begun to fail. Some fall by the way, and cannot be induced to rise; some simply stagger, and refuse to tug their chains. The whip curls round their backs in vain; there is nothing for a teamster to do but draw the yoke and let the poor creatures drop into the rear, where the wolves and ravens put an end to their miseries. The path is strewn with skeletons of ox and mule. Again and again we meet with trains in the Bitter Creek country, in which a third of the oxen are in hospital; that is to say, have been relieved from their labour, thrown on the flank to graze, or left behind on the chance of their recovery, perhaps in care of a lad. When many animals of a stock fall sick, the strain put on the healthy beasts becomes severe, and the whole caravan, unable to go forward, may have to camp for a week of rest in most unhealthy ground.

Lying between the two great ridges of the Rocky Mountains, the Bitter Creek country, a valley about the average height of Mons Pilatus above the sea, is, of course, intensely cold. The saying of the herdsmen is, that winter ends with July, and begins with August. Many of the mules and oxen die of frost, especially in the fall, when the burning sun of noon is suddenly exchanged for the icy winds of midnight. Frost comes upon the cattle unawares, with a soft seductive sense of comfort, so that they seem to bend their knees and close their eyes in perfect health; yet, when the morning dawns, it is seen that they will never rise again from their bed of sleep. It is much the same with men; who often lie down in their rugs and skins on the ground, a little numb, perhaps, in the feet; not miserably so, their toes being only just touched with the chill of ice; yet the more knowing hands among them feel that they will never find life and use in those feet again. I heard of one train captain, who, being careful of his men and teams, had put them up for the night, near Black Buttes, in a time of trouble with the Sioux; and who, being well clothed and mounted, had undertaken, in relief of another, to act as their sentinel and guard. All night he sat his pony in the cold; shivering a little, dozing a little; but on the rustling of a leaf, awake, alert, and watchful. When daylight came, and the camp began to stir, he shouted to one of his drivers, and would have drawn his foot from the leather rest, which serves the mountaineer instead of a stirrup; but his leg was stiff, and would not obey his will. In his surprise, he tried to raise the other leg, but the muscles once more refused to answer. When he was lifted down from the saddle, his legs were found to have been frozen to the knee; and after three days' agony he expired.

Nothing is more usual than to see men on the prairies and in the mountains who have lost either toes or fingers, bitten away by frost.

Hardly less trying to the mountaineers than frost and snow, are the sudden storms which rage and howl through these lofty plains. On my return from Salt Lake City across the Bitter Creek, a storm of snow, of sleet and hail, swept down upon us, right in our front, hitting us in the face like shot, and soaking us suddenly to the skin. At first we met it bravely, keeping our horses to the fore, and making a little progress, even in the teeth of this riotous squall. But the horses soon gave in. Terrified by the roaring wind, chilled by the smiting hail, they stood stone still; dogged, stolid, passive, utterly indifferent to the driver's voice and the driver's whip. Taught by his long experience, the driver knew when the brutes must have their way; he suddenly wheeled round, as though he was about to return, and setting the waggon to the fore, put his team under its lee, with their hindquarters only exposed to the pelting storm. In this position we remained three hours, until the swirl and tumult had gone by; after which we got down from the waggon, shook ourselves dry in the cold night air, and with the help of a little cognac and tobacco (taken as medicine) we resumed our journey.

A train of emigrants, which had to draw up near us, and await the tempest's passage, was not so lucky in arrangement as ourselves. The men had stopped their caravan as soon as the mules and horses had refused to move; but instead of bracing their frightened animals closer to the waggons, they had loosened their bands and suffered them to face the elements as they pleased. Some of them could not stand this freedom from the trace and curb. For a moment they stood still; they sniffed the air; they shook with panic; then, turning their faces from the wind, they pawed the wet ground, bent down their heads, and went off madly into space; a regular stampede, in the course of which many of the poor creatures would be sure to drop down dead from terror and exhaustion. We could not see the end of our neighbours' troubles, for the night came down between us and their camp, and on the instant slackening of the wind, we wheeled the waggon round, and trotted on our way. The emigrants would have to wait for dawn, to commence their search for the wandering mules and horses; some they would find in the nearer creeks, where they happened to first shelter from the driving storm; others they would have to follow over ridge and gully, many a long mile. Once in motion, with the hail and wind beating heavily on their backs, horses will never stop; will climb over mountains, rush into rivers, break through underwood, until the violence of nature has spent itself out. Then they will stand and shiver, perhaps droop and die.

Bullocks, like mules and horses, suffer from these storm-frights, and the experienced teamster of the plains will yoke them together, and lash them to the waggons whenever he sees the sign of a tempest coming on. Herding in a corral, hearing the voices of their drivers, they are less alarmed than when, loose and alone, they break into a stampede; yet even in a corral, with the song of the teamster in their ears, they shake and moan, lie down on the earth and cry, and not unfrequently die of fright.

In the midst of these terrors and confusions in a train — when the horses are either strayed or sick, when the boss is busy with his stock, when the teamsters are exhausted by fatigue and hunger — the road-agents generally fall on the corral and find it an easy prey.

Road-agent is the name applied in the mountains to a ruffian who has given up honest work in the store, in the mine, in the ranch, for the perils and profits of the highway. Many ruined traders, broken gamblers, unsuccessful diggers, take to the road, plundering trains of their goods, robbing emigrants of their mules, and sometimes venturing to attack the mail. They are all well armed, some of them are certain shots. No fear of man, and no respect for woman, restrain these plunderers from committing the most atrocious crimes. Their hands are raised against every one who may be expected to have a dollar in his purse. Every law which they can break, they have already broken; every outrage which they can effect, they have probably effected; so that their dregs of life are already due to justice; and nothing they can do will add to the load of guilt which they already bear. These plunderers, who roam about the tracks in bands of three or five, of ten or twenty, sometimes of thirty or forty, are far more terrible to the merchant and the emigrant than either Sioux or Ute. The Sioux is but a savage, whom the white man has a chance of daunting by his pride, of deceiving by his craft; but his brother on the road, himself perhaps a trader, a train-man in his happier days, can see through every wile, and measure with a glance both his weakness and his strength.

Many men, known to have been road-agents, suspected of being still connected with the bands, are at large; this man keeping a grog-shop, that man living in a ranch, the other man driving the mail. In this free western country you cannot ask many questions as to character. A steady wrist, a quick eye, a prompt invention, are of more importance in a servant than the very best testimonials from his recent place. Life is too rough for the nicer rules to come into play. I saw a fellow in Denver whose name is as well known in Colorado as that of Dick Turpin in Yorkshire. He is said to have murdered half-a-dozen men; he is free to come and go, to buy and sell; no one molests him; fear of his companions, and of men who live by crimes like his, being strong enough to daunt, for a time, even the Vigilance Committee and their daring Sheriff. On my return through the Bitter Creek country, I had the honour of riding in the mountain waggon with an old road-agent, who laughed and joked over his exploits, caring not a jot for either sheriff or judge. One of his stories ran as follows. He and a wretch like himself, being out on the road, had been rather lucky, and having got a thousand dollars in greenbacks in their pouch, they were making for Denver city, where they hoped to enjoy their plunder, when they saw in the distance five mounted men, whom my companion said he knew at once to be part of a gang in which he had formerly served on terms of share and share. "We are lost now," he said to his companion in crime; "these men will rob us of our greenbacks, possibly shoot us into the bargain, so as not to leave a witness of their deed alive."

"We shall see," replied his more crafty friend. "I know them, and have been out with them; we must get over them as broken-down wretches."

Smearing themselves with dirt, dragging a long face, and looking hungry and miserable, they met the five horsemen with the cry, "Give us five dollars, captain; we are broken down and trying to get on to Denver, where we'll find some friends; give us five dollars!" This cry of distress went straight to the highwayman's heart. He tossed my companion the greenbacks, telling him to be mum, and then dashed on in front of his more suspicious comrades.

Not long ago, a party of these road-agents robbed the imperial mail, with circumstances of unusual harshness, even in the mountains. The story of the crime is in everybody's mouth as that of the Portliff Canyon murder; and is here told, mainly from the murderer's confession to Sheriff Wilson.

Frank Williams, a man of bad character, but a good whip, a good shot, an experienced mountaineer, got employment as a driver on the Overland route. On one of this man's visits to Salt Lake he made the acquaintance of one Parker of Atchison, a trader who had been doing business in the Mormon city, and was about to return with his gains to the River town. M'Causland of Virginia, and two other merchants, having with them a large sum of money in gold dust, were proposing to go back with Parker in the mail, for their mutual safety. These names and facts Parker told Frank Williams as they drank together, at the same time asking his advice in the matter as a driver and a friend. Under Frank Williams' suggestion the four men took their places in the stage; they were the only passengers that day; and they made a prosperous journey until they arrived in Portliff Canyon, where Parker found Frank, who had gone back from Salt Lake City to his accustomed drive.

In that canyon they were murdered. In a narrow

gorge of the pass Frank let his whip fall to the ground; he stopped the coach, and ran backwards to pick it up; when a volley of shot came rattling into the mail, and three of the men inside of it fell dead. Eight fellows in masks rushed up to the mail, pulled out the dead and dying, and seized upon their boxes with the gold dust and the greenbacks. Parker was hurt, though not to his death; and on seeing Williams come back, pistol in hand, he cried out to his friend to spare his life: "I am only hipped; help me, Frank, and I shall do!" Frank put the pistol to his friend's head and blew his brains into the air; not daring to allow one witness of his crime to remain alive. He then drove into the station, where he reported that the mail had been robbed, the passengers killed. Two men went out with him to find the dead bodies, and a search was made from Denver to Salt Lake for the assassins. No suspicion fell upon Frank, until a few weeks after the robbery and murder, when news was brought to Sheriff Wilson by a thief, that Frank Williams had left his place on the mail line, and was spending his money rather freely in the Gentile grog-shops of Salt Lake. Bob instantly took steps to have him watched in those dens; but while he was setting his spies in motion, Williams suddenly appeared in the streets of Denver, close to that cotton-tree on which the Sheriff looks down from his auctioneer's throne. Before he had been a day in Denver, he had bought for himself and his boon companions seven new suits of clothes, had hired a brothel, and treated nearly every ruffian in the town to drink.

One evening he was seized by Wilson, who conducted him to a midnight sitting of the Vigilance Committee. What took place in that sitting is unknown; the names of those who were present can be only guessed; but it was evident to every one next day that Frank Williams had been found guilty of some atrocious crime. Men who got up early that morning had seen his body dangling from a buggy-pole in Main Street.

CHAPTER XV.

Descent of the Mountains.

AFTER passing Fort Bridger the descent becomes quick, abrupt, and verdant. The track is still rough, stony, unmade; here running over round crests, there cutting into deep canyons, anon toiling through troughs of sand; but on the whole we go dropping down from the high plateau of the Sierras, where Nature is dry and sterile, seemingly unfit for the occupation of man, into deep ravines and narrow dales, in which the wild sage gives place to tall, rank grass. A little scrub begins to show itself in the clefts and hollows; dwarf oak and maple now putting on their autumnal garb of pink and gold. Stunted pines and cedars become a feature in the landscape; a noise of water babbles up from the glens; long serpentine fringes of balsam and willow show the courses of the descending creeks. We rattle, in the fading light, through Muddy Creek, and roll, in the early darkness, past Quaking Asp, — startled, as we come round the ledge of a sharp hill, to see before us a mighty flame, as though the valley in our front, the hill-side on our flank, were all on fire. It is a Mormon camp. About a hundred waggons, corralled, in the usual way, for defence against Utes and Snakes, are halted in a dark valley, where rocks and crests pile high into the heavens, shutting out the stars. In front of each waggon burns a huge fire; men and women, boys and girls, are gathered round these fires; some eating their supper, some singing brisk songs, others again dancing; oxen, mules, horses, stand about in happy confusion of group and colour; dogs sleep round the fires or bark at the mail; and through all this wild, unexpected scene, clash the cymbals, horns, and trumpets of a band. Though we are still high up in the mountains, we feel, as it were, already on the borders of the Salt Lake Eden, that home of the Latter-Day Saints, to which the weaver is called from Manchester, the peasant from Llandudno, the cobbler from Whitechapel.

An hour later we drop into Bear River station, kept by acting-bishop Myers, an English member of the Mormon Church; a dignitary who has hitherto limited his rights over the weaker sex to the wedding of two wives. One wife lives with him at Bear River; one hired help, a young English woman on a visit (and I fear in some little peril of the heart), with two or three men, his servants, make up this bishop's flock and household. The wife is a lady; simple, elegant, bewitching; who, while we rinse the dust from our throats and dash cold water about our heads and faces, hastily and daintily sets herself to cook our food. Tired and hungry as we are, this Myers appears to us the very model of a working bishop for a working world. At Oxford he would count for little, in the House of Lords for nothing. His words are not choice, his intonation is not good and musical; he hardly (I will not answer for it) knows a Greek particle by sight; but he seems to know very well how a good man should receive the hungry and weary who are cast down at his door on a frosty night. After poking up the stove, heaping wood upon the fire, chopping up a side of mutton (it is the first fresh meat we have seen for days), he runs out of doors to haul water from the well, and puts straw into our coach that our feet may be kept warm in the coming frost. From him we get genuine tea, good bread, even butter; not sage-tea, hot dough, and a pinch of salt. The chops are delicious; and the bishop's elegant wife and her ladylike friend, by the grace and courtesy with which they serve the table, turn a common mountain meal into a banquet.

We leave Bear River with respect for one phase of the working episcopacy founded by Brigham Young.

In the night we pass by Hanging Rock and roll down Echo Canyon; a ravine of rocks and nooks, surprising, lovely, fantastic, when they are seen under the light of luminous autumn stars. Early morning brings us to Weber River, where we break our fasts on hot-bake and leather; early day to Coalville, the first Mormon village on our road; a settlement built of wooden sheds, in the midst of rude gardens and patches of corn-fields, hardly redeemed from that wild waste of nature, in the midst of which a few Utes and Bannocks hunted the elk and scalped each other not a score of years since. Coal is found here; also a little water, a little wood. We glance with quick eyes into the houses, some of which stand in groups and rows, as we learn from our driver that those wooden cottages which have two or more doors, are the houses of elders who have married two or more wives. We think of the arid sweeps through which we have just come; of our six days' journey among rocky passes and mountain slopes; and gaze with wonder on the courage, industry, fanaticism, which could have been induced, by any teaching, by any promise, to attack this desolate valley, with a view to making out of it a habitation fit for m n. But here is Coalville; a town in the hills, at least the beginning of a town; placed in a gorge where engineers and explorers had declared it utterly impossible for either man or beast to live. Patches of corn run down to the little creek. Oxen graze on the hill-sides. Dogs guard the farm-houses. Hogs grub into the soil; chickens hop among the sheaves; and horses stand in the court-yards. Rosy children, with their blue eyes and flaxen curls telling of their pure English blood, play before the gates and tumble in the straw. Girls of nine or ten years are milking cows; boys of the same age are driving teams; women are cooking, washing; men are digging potatoes, gathering in fruit, chopping and sawing planks. Every man seems busy, every place prosperous, though the ravine was but yesterday a desert of dust and stones. From among the green shrubs a neat little chapel peeps out.

Lower down the valleys the scene expands, and herds of cattle dot the wide sweeps of grass. We pass Kimball's Hotel — a station of the Overland mail — kept by one of Heber Kimball's sons; a man of some wealth, living out here in the lonely hills, with his sheep, his cattle, and his three wives; professing the Mormon creed, though he is said to have been drummed out of the society of Salt Lake for tipsiness and rioting in the public streets. Sharp justice, as we hear, is meted out by the Saints upon offenders; no claims of blood, however high and near, being suffered to protect a criminal from the sentence of his church.

At Mountain Dell, the house of Bishop Hardy, a man having eight wives, three of whom live with him in this mountain shed, we see a little Ute Indian, who has been reclaimed from his tribe, made into a faithful Mormon and a good boy; a shrewd lad, who seems to know the difference between dining off wolf and off mutton, and who hates the red-skins, his brethren in the war-paint, with all his soul. From one of the bishop's wives we learn that he was bought, as a papoose, from his father for a few dollars; that he is a sharp fellow, and works very well when he is made to do so; that he is lazy by nature, and apt to lie much in the sun; that he is slow at books and learning; but takes easily to horses, and drives a team very well. In fact, he is capable of being raised into a white man's servant, and trained, at much cost and care, to fetch in wood and water for the white man's use.

The Mormons have a peculiar view about the red men, whom they regard as a branch of the Hebrew people, who migrated from Palestine to North America in their days of power and righteousness, while they yet held the priesthood in their hands. When, through the sin of disobedience, they lost their priesthood, they lost, along with that sacred office, their white colour, their bright intelligence, their noble physiognomy. According to the Mormons, some rags and tatters of their early faith — of their ancient institutions — still remain to these remnants of Israel; their belief in one Great Spirit; their division into tribes; their plurality of wives. But the curse of God is upon them and upon their seed. They come of a sacred race, — but a sacred race now lying under the stern reproof of Heaven. "In time — in God's own time," said Young to me, in a subsequent conversation, "they will be recalled into a state of grace: they will then cease to do evil and learn to do good; they will settle down in cities; they will become white in colour; and they will act as a nation of priests."

The change will, indeed, be great that transforms a Pawnee and a Ute into the likeness of Aaron and of Joshua.

Before the war broke out, and slavery was banished as an institution from the American soil, the Saints had passed a territorial law permitting the purchase of boys and girls from the Indians, with a view to their being baptized into the Church and taught useful trades. Ute and Snake are only too ready to sell their infants; and many young redskins, bought under that law, are still to be found in these valleys. Of course they are now free as the whites, and far more lazy, treacherous, and wicked.

The bishop's wife, having had her eyes opened by many trials, has come to have little faith in the government plan for reclaiming Utes and Bannocks. She sees that a curse is on them and on their seed; she hopes that when the time shall come for that curse to be removed, the red man will be made capable of thrift, of labour, of salvation; but that removal, she owns to herself, must be the work of God, not that of man.

A long steep canyon, nine or ten miles in length, — with fringe of verdure and beck of water running through it; the verdure feeding cattle, the water working mills, — opens a way from Mountain Dell into the Salt Lake Basin, which we come upon suddenly, and by a sort of surprise, on turning a projecting mountain ledge.

The scene now in front of us, from whatever point of view it may be taken, is one of the half-dozen pure and perfect landscapes which the earth can show. No wonder that the poor emigrant from a Liverpool cellar, from a Blackwall slum, exalted, as his vision must be, with religious fervour, and by sharp privation, looks down upon it as a terrestrial Paradise.

Lying at the foot of these snowy ranges of the Wasatch mountains, spreads the great plain, far away into the unseen vistas of the north; the whole expanse of valley filled with a golden haze of surprising richness, the effect of a tropical sunshine streaming over fields sown thick with sun-flowers, like an English field with buttercups, and over multitudinous lakelets, pools, and streams: to the left soar into the clouds and curl round the Great Salt Lake a chain of mountains, which the Indians call Oquirrh. In our front lies the sparkling city, the New Jerusalem, in its bowers of trees; beyond that city flows the Jordan, bearing the fresh waters of Utah through the plains into Salt Lake, which darkens and cools the great valley, with its amplitudes of blue. From the lake itself, which is a hundred miles broad, a hundred and fifty miles long, spring two islands, purple and mountainous; Antelope Island (now called Church Island) and Stansbury Island; while, on either side, and beyond the blue waters of the lake itself, run chains of irregular and picturesque heights, the barren sierras of Utah and Nevada.

The air is soft and sweet; southern in its odour, northern in its freshness. Cool winds come down from the Wasatch peaks; in which drifts of snow and frozen pools lie all through the summer months. So clear is the atmosphere, that Black Rock, on the Salt Lake, twenty-five miles distant, seems but a few hundred yards in our front, and crests which stand sixty miles apart, appear to our sight as though they were peaks of a single range.

Lower down in the valley the golden haze steeps everything in its own delicious light. The city appears to be one vast park or garden, in which you count innumerable masses of dark green trees, with a white kiosk, a chapel, a court-house, sprinkled about it here and there. Above it, on a bank of higher land, is the camp; a cluster of white tents and shanties; from which a Gentile government watches suspiciously the doings of men in this city of the Saints. But the camp itself adds picture to the scene; a bar of colour to the landscape of yellow, white, and green.

CHAPTER XVI.

The New Jerusalem.

A DREAM of the night, helped by a rush of water from the hill-side, (not larger than the Xenil, which gave life to Granada, and changed the barren vega into a garden,) fixed the site of the New Jerusalem. Brigham Young tells me, that when coming over the mountains, in search of a new home for his people, he saw, in a vision of the night, an angel standing on a conical hill, pointing to a spot of ground on which the new Temple must be built. Coming down into this basin of Salt Lake, he first sought for the cone which he had seen in his dream; and when he had found it, he noticed a stream of fresh hill-water flowing at its base, which he called the City Creek. Elder George Smith, and a few of the pioneers, led this creek through and through a patch of likely soil, into which they then stuck potatoes; and having planted these bulbs, they took a few steps northward, marked out the Temple site, and drew a great square line about it. That square block, ten acres in extent, is the heart of the city, the Mormon holy place, the haram of this young Jerusalem of the West.

The site of the new city was laid between the two great lakes, Utah Lake and Salt Lake — like the town of Interlachen between Brienz and Thun — though the distances are here much greater, the two inland seas of Utah being real seas when compared against the two charming lakelets in the Bernese Alps. A river now called the Jordan flows from Utah into Salt Lake; but it skirts the town only, and lying low down in the valley, is useless, as yet, for irrigation. Young has a plan for constructing a canal from Utah lake to the city, by way of the lower benches of the Wasatch chain; a plan which will cost much money, and fertilise enormous sweeps of barren soil. If Salt Lake City is left to extend itself in peace, the canal will soon be dug; and the bench, now covered with stones, with sand, and a little wild sage, will be changed into vineyards and gardens.

The city, which covers, we are told, three thousand acres of land, between the mountains and the river, is laid out in blocks of ten acres each. Each block is divided into lots of one acre and a quarter; this quantity of land being considered enough for an ordinary cottage and garden.

As yet, the Temple is unbuilt; the foundations are well laid, of massive granite; and the work is of a kind that bids fair to last; but the Temple block is covered with temporary buildings and erections — the old tabernacle, the great bowery, the new tabernacle, the temple foundations. A high wall encloses these edifices; a poor wall, without art, without strength; more like a mud wall than the great work which surrounds the temple platform on Moriah. When the works are finished, the enclosure will be trimmed and planted, so as to offer shady walks and a garden of flowers.

The Temple block gives form to the whole city. From each side of it starts a street, a hundred feet in width, going out on the level plain, and in straight lines into space. Streets of the same width, and parallel to these, run north and south, east and west; each planted with locust and ailantus trees, cooled by two running streams of water from the hill-side. These streets go up north, towards the bench, and nothing but the lack of people prevents them from travelling onward, south and west, to the lakes, which they already reach on paper, and in the imaginations of the more fervid saints.

Main Street runs along the Temple front; a street of offices, of residences, and of trade. Originally, it was meant for a street of the highest rank, and bore the name of East Temple Street; upon it stood, besides the Temple itself, the Council house, the Tithing office, the dwellings of Young, Kimball, Wells, the three chief officers of the Mormon church. It was once amply watered and nobly planted; but commerce has invaded the precincts of the modern temple, as it invaded those of the old; and the power of Brigham Young has broken and retreated before that of the money-dealers and the vendors of meat and raiment. Banks, stores, offices, hotels, — all the conveniences of modern life, — are springing up in Main Street; trees have in many parts been cut down, for the sake of loading and unloading goods; the trim little gardens, full of peach-trees and apple-trees, bowering the adobe cottages in their midst, have given way to shop-fronts and to hucksters' stalls. In the business portion, Main Street is wide, dusty, unpaved, unbuilt; a street showing the three stages through which every American city has to pass; the log-shanty, the adobe cot (in places where clay and fuel can be easily obtained, this stage is one of brick), and the stone house. Many of the best houses are still of wood; more are of adobe, the sun-dried bricks once used in Babylonia and in Egypt, and still used everywhere in Mexico and California; a few are of red stone, and even granite. The Temple is being built of granite from a neighbouring hill. The Council house is of red stone; as are many of the great magazines, such as Godbe's, Jennings', Gilbert's, Clawson's; magazines in which you find everything for sale, as in a Turkish bazaar, from candles and champagne, down to gold dust, cotton prints, tea, pen-knives, canned meats, and mouse-traps. The smaller shops, the ice-cream houses, the saddlers, the barbers, the restaurants, the hotels, and all the better class of dwellings, are of sun-dried bricks; a good material in this dry and sunny climate; bright to the eye, cosy in winter, cool in summer; though such houses are apt to crumble away in a shower of rain. A few shanties, remnants of the first emigration, still remain in sight. Lower down, towards the south, where the street runs off into infinite space, the locust and ailantus trees re-appear.

In its busy, central portion, nothing hints the difference between Main Street in Salt Lake City, and the chief thoroughfare, say, of Kansas, Leavenworth, and Denver, except the absence of grog-shops, lager-beer saloons, and bars. The hotels have no bars; the streets have no betting-houses, no gaming-tables, no brothels, no drinking-places. In my hotel — "The Salt Lake" — kept by Col. Little, one of the Mormon elders, I cannot buy a glass of beer, a flask of wine. No house is now open for the sale of drink (though the Gentiles swear they will have one open in a few weeks); and the table of the hotel is served at morning, noon, and night, with tea. In this absence of public solicitation to sip either claret-cobbler, whisky-bourbon, Tom and Jerry, mint-julep, eye-opener, fix-up, or any other Yankee deception in the shape of liquor, the city is certainly very much unlike Leavenworth, and the River towns, where every third house in a street appears to be a drinking den. Going past the business quarter, we return to the first ideas of Young in planting his new home; the familiar lines of acacias grow by the becks; the cottages stand back from the road-side twenty or thirty-feet; the peach-trees, apple-trees and vines, tricked out with roses and sun-flowers, smother up the roofs.

Right and left from Main Street, crossing it, parallel to it, lie a multitude of streets, each like its fellow; a hard, dusty road, with tiny becks, and rows of locust, cotton-wood, and philarea, and the building-land laid down in blocks. In each block stands a cottage, in the midst of fruit trees. Some of these houses are of goodly appearance as to size and style, and would let for high rentals in the Isle of Wight. Others are mere cots of four or five rooms, in which the polygamous families, should they ever quarrel, would find it difficult to form a ring and fight. In some of these orchards you see two, three houses; pretty Swiss cottages, like many in St. John's Wood as to gable, roof, and paint: these are the dwellings of different wives. "Whose houses are these?" we ask a lad in East Temple Street, pointing to some pretty-looking villas. "They belong," says he, "to Brother Kimball's family." Here, on the bench, in the highest part of the city, is Elder Hiram Clawson's garden; a lovely garden, red with delicious peaches, plums, and apples, on which, through the kindness of his youngest wife, we have been hospitably fed during our sojourn with the Saints; a large house stands in front, in which live his first and second wives with their nurseries of twenty children. But what is yon dainty white bower in the corner, with its little gate and its smother of roses and creepers? That is the house of the youngest wife, Alice, a daughter of Brigham Young. She has a nest of her own, apart from the other women, — a nest in which she lives with her four little boys, and where she is supposed to have as much of her own way with her lord, as the daughter of a Sultan enjoys in the harem of a Pasha. Elder Naisbit, one of the Mormon poets, an English convert to the faith as it is in Joseph, lives with his two wives and their brood of young children on the high ground opposite to Elder Clawson, in a very pretty mansion, something like a cottage on the Under Cliff. Much of the city is only green glade and orchard waiting for the people who are yet to come and fill it with the pride of life.

In First South Street stand the Theatre and the

City hall, both fine structures, and for Western America remarkable in style.

The City hall is used as head-quarters of police, and as a court of justice. The Mormon police are swift and silent, with their eyes in every corner, their grip on every rogue. No fact, however slight, appears to escape their notice. A Gentile friend of mine, going through the dark streets at night towards the theatre, spoke to a Mormon lady of his acquaintance whom he overtook; next day a gentleman called at his hotel, and warned him not to speak with a Mormon woman in the dark streets unless her father should be with her. In the winter months there are usually seven or eight hundred miners in Salt Lake City, young Norse gods of the Denver stamp; every man with a bowie-knife in his belt, a revolver in his hand, clamouring for beer and whisky, for gaming-tables and lewd women, comforts which are strictly denied to them by these Saints. The police have all these violent spirits to repress; that they hold them in decent order with so little bloodshed is the wonder of every western governor and judge. William Gilpin, governor elect of Colorado, and Robert Wilson, sheriff of Denver and justice of the peace, have nothing but praise to give these stern and secret, but most able and effective ministers of police.

With this court of justice we have scarcely made acquaintance. A few nights ago we met the judge, who kindly asked us to come and see his court; but while we were chatting in his ante-room, before the cases were called, some one whispered in his ear that we were members of the English bar, on which he slipped out of sight, and adjourned his court. This judge, when he is not sitting on the Bench, is engaged in vending drugs across a counter in Main Street; and as we know where to find him in his store, we sometimes drop in for soda-water and a cigar; but we have not yet been able to fix a time for seeing his method of administering justice at Salt Lake.

The city has two sulphur-springs, over which Brigham Young has built wooden shanties. One bath is free. The water is refreshing and relaxing, the heat 92°.

No beggar is seen in the streets; scarcely ever a tipsy man; and the drunken fellow, when you see one, is always either a miner or a soldier — of course a Gentile. No one seems poor. The people are quiet and civil, far more so than is usual in these western parts. From the presence of trees, of water, and of cattle, the streets have a pastoral character, seen in no other city of the mountains and the plains. Here, standing under the green locust trees, is an ox come home for the night; yonder is a cow at a gate being milked by a child. Light mountain-waggons stand about, and the sun-burnt emigrants, who have just come in from the prairies, thankful for shade and water, sit under the acacias, and dabble their feet in the running creeks.

More than all other streets, perhaps, Main Street, as the business quarter, offers picture after picture to an artist's eye; most of all when an emigrant-train is coming in from the plains. Such a scene is before me now; for the train which we passed in the gorge above Bear River has just arrived, with sixty waggons, four hundred bullocks, six hundred men, women, and children, all English and Welsh. The waggons fill the street: some of the cattle are lying down in the hot sun; the men are eager and excited, having finished their long journey across the sea, across the States, across the prairies, across the mountains; the women and little folks are scorched and wan; dirt, fatigue, privation, give them a wild, unearthly look; and you would hardly recognise in this picturesque and ragged group the sober Monmouth farmer, the clean Woolwich artisan, the smart London smith. Mule-teams are being unloaded at the stores. Miners from Montana and Idaho, in huge boots and belts, are loafing about. A gang of Snake Indians, with their long hair, their scant drapery, and their proud reserve, are cheapening the dirtiest and cheapest lots. Yon fellow in the broad sombrero, dashing up the dust with his wiry little horse, is a New Mexican; here comes a heavy Californian swell; and there, in the blue uniform, go two officers from the camp.

The air is wonderfully pure and bright. Rain seldom falls in the valley, though storms occur in the mountains almost daily; a cloud coming up in the western hills, rolling along the crests, and threatening the city with a deluge; but when breaking into wind and showers, it seems to run along the hill-tops into the Wasatch chain, and sail away eastward into the snowy range.

CHAPTER XVII.

The Mormon Theatre.

THE playhouse has an office and a service in this Mormon city higher than the churches would allow to it in London, Paris, and New York. Brigham Young is an original in many ways; he is the high-priest of what claims to be a new dispensation; yet he has got his theatre into perfect order, before he has raised his Temple foundations above the ground.

That the drama had a religious origin, and that the stage has been called a school of manners, every one is aware. Young feels inclined to go back upon all first principles; in family life to those of Abraham, in social life to those of Thespis. Priests invented both the ancient and the modern stages; and if experience shows as strongly in Salt Lake City as in New York, that people love to be light and merry — to laugh and glow — why should their teachers neglect the thousand opportunities offered by a play, of getting them to laugh in the right places, to glow at the proper things? Why should Young not preach moralities from the stage? Why should he not train his actors and his actresses to be models of good conduct, of correct pronunciation, and of taste in dress? Why should he not try to reconcile religious feeling with pleasure?

Brigham Young may be either right or wrong in

his ideas of the uses to which a playhouse may be turned in a city where they have no high schools and colleges as yet; but he is bent on trying his experiment to an issue; for this purpose he has built a model theatre, and he is now making an effort to train a model company.

Outside, his theatre is a rough Doric edifice, in which the architect has contrived to produce a certain effect by very simple means; inside, it is light and airy, having no curtains and no boxes, save two in the proscenium, with light columns to divide the tiers, and having no other decoration than pure white paint and gold. The pit, rising sharply from the orchestra, so that every one seated on its benches can see and hear to advantage, is the choicest part of the house. All these benches are let to families; and here the principal elders and bishops may be seen every play-night, surrounded by their wives and children, laughing and clapping like boys at a pantomime. Yon rocking-chair, in the centre of the pit, is Young's own seat; his place of pleasure, in the midst of his Saints. When he chooses to occupy his private box, one of his wives, perhaps Eliza the Poetess, Harriet the Pale, or Amelia the Magnificent, rocks herself in his chair while laughing at the play. Round about that chair, as the place of honour, cluster the benches of those who claim to stand nearest to their prophet: of Heber Kimball, first councillor; of Daniel Wells, second councillor and general-in-chief; of George A. Smith, apostle and historian of the church; of George Q. Cannon, apostle; of Edward Hunter, presiding bishop; of

Elder Stenhouse, editor of the 'Daily Telegraph;' and of a host of less brilliant Mormon lights.

In the sides of the proscenium nestle two private boxes; one is reserved for the Prophet, when he pleases to be alone, or wishes to have a gossip with some friend; the other is given up to the girls who have to play during the night, but who are not engaged in the immediate business of the piece. As a rule, every one's pleasure is considered in this model playhouse; and I can answer, on the part of Miss Adams, Miss Alexander, and other young artists, that this appropriation to their sole use of a private box, into which they can run at all times, in any dress, without being seen, is considered by them as a very great comfort.

Through the quick eye and careful hand of his manager, Hiram Clawson, the President may be congratulated on having made his playhouse into something coming near to that which he conceives a playhouse should be. Everything in front of the footlights is in keeping; peace and order reign in the midst of fun and frolic. Neither within the doors nor about them, do you find the riot of our own Lyceum and Drury Lane; no loose women, no pickpockets, no ragged boys and girls, no drunken and blaspheming men. As a Mormon never drinks spirits, and rarely smokes tobacco, the only dissipation in which you find these hundreds of hearty creatures indulging their appetites, is that of sucking a peach. Short plays are in vogue in this theatre, just as short sermons are the rule in yon tabernacle. The curtain, which rises at eight, comes down about half-past ten; and as the Mormon fashion is for people to sup before going out, they retire to rest the moment they get home, never suffering their amusements to infringe on the labours of the coming day. Your bell rings for breakfast at six o'clock.

But the chief beauties of this model playhouse lie behind the scenes; in the ample space, the perfect light, the scrupulous cleanliness of every part. I am pretty well acquainted with green-rooms and side wings in Europe; but I have never seen, not in Italian and Austrian theatres, so many delicate arrangements for the privacy and comfort of ladies and gentlemen as at Salt Lake. The green-room is a real drawing-room. The scene-painters have their proper studios; the dressers and decorators have immense magazines. Every lady, however small her part in the play, has a dressing-room to herself.

Young understands that the true work of reform in a playhouse must begin behind the scenes: that you must elevate the actor before you can purify the stage. To this end, he not only builds dressing-rooms and a private box for the ladies who have to act, but he places his daughters on the stage as an example and encouragement to others. Three of these young sultanas, Alice, Emily, and Zina, are on the stage. With Alice, the youngest wife of Elder Clawson, I have had the honour to make an acquaintance, which might be called a friendship, and from her lips I have learned a good deal as to her father's ideas about stage reform. "I am not myself very fond of playing," she said to me one day as we sat at dinner — not in these words, perhaps, but to this effect — "but my father desires that my sisters and myself should act sometimes, as he does not think it right to ask any poor man's child to do anything which his own children would object to do." Her dislike to playing, as she afterwards told me, arose from a feeling that Nature had given her no abilities for acting well; she was fond of going to see a good piece, and seldom omitted being present when she had not to play. Brigham Young has to create, as well as to reform, the stage of Salt Lake City; and the chief trouble of a manager who is seven hundred miles from the next theatre, must always be with his artists. Talent for the work does not grow in every field, like a sunflower and a peach-tree; it must be sought for in nooks and corners; now in a shoe-shop, anon in a dairy, then in a counting-house; but wherever the talent may be found, Young cannot think of asking any young girl to do a thing which it is supposed that a daughter of his own would scorn.

In New York, in St. Louis, in Chicago, nobody would assert that the stage is a school of virtue, that acting is a profession which a sober man would like his daughters to adopt. Young does not blind himself to the fact that in claiming the theatre as a school of morals, he has to fight against a social judgment. An odour of vice, as of a poisonous weed, infects the air of a playhouse everywhere; though nowhere less offensively than in American towns. Against this evil, much of it the consequence of bad traditions, he offers up, as it were, a part of himself — his children; the only persons in Salt

Lake City who could really do this cleansing work. In this way, Alice and Zina may be regarded as two priestly virgins who have been placed on the public stage to purify it by their presence from an ancient but unnecessary stain.

Young, and his agent Clawson, are bestowing much care upon the education of Miss Adams, a young lady who has everything to learn except the art of being lovely; also upon that of Miss Alexander, a girl who, besides being pretty and piquant, has genuine ability for her work. A story, which shows that Young has a feeling for humour, has been told me, of which Miss Alexander is the heroine. A starring actor from San Francisco fell into desperate love for her, and went up to the President's house for leave to address her. "Ha! my good fellow," said the Prophet; "I have seen you play 'Hamlet' very well, and 'Julius Cæsar' pretty well, but you must not aspire to Alexander!"

We saw Brigham Young for the first time in his private box. A large head, broad, fair face, with blue eyes, light brown hair, good nose, and merry mouth; a man, plainly dressed, in black coat and pantaloons, white waistcoat and cravat, gold studs and sleeve-links, English in build and looks, — but English of the middle class and of a provincial town; such was the Mormon prophet, pope, and king, as we first saw him in the theatre among his people. A lady, one of his wives, whom we afterwards came to know as Amelia, sat with him in the box; she, too, was dressed in a quiet English style; and now and then she eyed the audience from behind her curtain, through an opera-glass, as English ladies are apt to do at home. She was pretty, and appeared to us then rather pensive and poetical.

The pit was almost filled with girls; on many benches sat a dozen damsels in a row; children of Kimball, Cannon, Smith, and Wells; in some places twenty or thirty girls were grouped together. Young, as he told me himself, has forty-eight living children, some of whom are grown up and married; and, since he sets the fashion of attending this theatre among his people, it is only right that he should encourage his children to appear, both before the foot-lights and behind them. Alice is the young lady married to Clawson. Zina, whom we have seen play Mrs. Musket in the farce of "My Husband's Ghost," is a lady-like girl, tall, full in figure, moon-faced (as the Orientals say), not much of an artist. Emily we have also seen; Elder Clawson is said to be courting her. I am told that the flame is mutual; and that Emily is not unlikely to be gathered home to her sister Alice. Gentile rumour — fond of toying with the domestic secrets of the President's family — says that Alice is not happy with her lord; but this is one of those Gentile rumours which I can almost swear is false. One day, last week, I had the pleasure of taking Sister Alice down to dinner, of talking with her for a long evening, and of seeing and romping with her four brave boys. A brighter, merrier woman, I have rarely seen; and I noted, as a peculiarity in her, not common in either eastern or western America, that she always addressed her husband by his baptismal name of Hiram. American ladies almost everywhere speak to their husbands as Mr. Jones and Mr. Smith, not as William and George. The perils of a double alliance with the Mormon pope are said to be great; envy among the elders, collision with the Gentiles, jealousy at Camp Douglas, hostility in Washington; but Elder Clawson is said to be ready to take his chance with Sister Emily, as he has done with Alice, answering, as the Mormons put it, Washington theories by Deseret facts.

The first piece we saw was "Charles the Twelfth." Where Adam Brock warns his daughter, Eudiga, against military sparks, the whole pit of young ladies crackled off into girlish laughter; the reference being taken to Camp Douglas and the United States officers stationed there, many of whom were in the house, and heartily enjoyed the fun. This play happens to be full of allusions to soldiers and their amours, and every word of these allusions was appropriated and applied by the Saints to their local politics. The interference of these United States officers and soldiers with the Mormon women is a very sore point with the Saints, some of their wives having, it is said, been seduced and carried off. Young spoke to me with indignation of such proceedings, though he did not name the offenders as connected with the camp. "They cause us trouble," he said; "they intrude into our affairs, and even into our families; we cannot stand such things; and when they are guilty we make them bite the dust." I thought of all that I had ever heard about Porter Rockwell and his Danite band; but I only smiled and waited for the President to go on. He quickly added, "I never had any trouble of this sort in my own family."

When Charles the Twelfth referred to the amours of his officers, it was good fun to see the Prophet rolling back in his chair, convulsed with merriment, while the more staid Amelia eyed the audience through her opera-glass.

CHAPTER XVIII.

The Temple.

WHAT the Theatre is to the social life of this people, the Temple is to its religious life. One symbolises the enjoyment of the present world; the other typifies the glories of a world to come. The playhouse has been raised and opened because its service is concerned with the things which cannot wait; the Temple is proceeding slowly, block being piled on block with the care and leisure of a work designed to last for ever.

These Mormons profess to have so much religion in their blood and bone, that they can easily dispense, on occasion, with religious forms. A few days ago, I happened to hear the first discourse of Brigham Young to a band of emigrants; the practical character of which would have taken me by surprise, but that my previous intercourse with him had in some degree prepared me for it.

"Brothers and sisters in the Lord Jesus Christ," he said, in substance, "you have been chosen from the world by God, and sent through His grace into this valley of the mountains, to help in building up His kingdom. You are faint and weary from your march. Rest, then, for a day, for a second day, should you need it; then rise up, and see how you will live. Don't bother yourselves much about your religious duties; you have been chosen for this work, and God will take care of you in it. Be of good cheer. Look about this valley into which you have been called. Your first duty is to learn how to grow a cabbage, and along with this cabbage an onion, a tomato, a sweet potato; then how to feed a pig, to build a house, to plant a garden, to rear cattle, and to bake bread; in one word, your first duty is to live. The next duty — for those who, being Danes, French, and Swiss, cannot speak it now — is to learn English; the language of God, the language of the Book of Mormon, the language of these Latter Days. These things you must do first; the rest will be added to you in proper seasons. God bless you; and the peace of our Lord Jesus Christ be with you."

The Temple is not forgotten; in fact, no people on the earth devote more money to their religious edifices and services than the Mormons. A tenth of all produce — often much more — is cheerfully given up to the church; but the first thought of a convert, the first counsel of an elder, is always, that the Saint shall look upon labour, labour of the hand and brain, and most of all labour of the hand, as the appointed sacrifice through which, by God's own law, a man shall be purged from sin and shall attain everlasting peace. All the passions which another sect throws into polemics, the Mormons put into work. They do not shun discussion by the tongue; in fact, they are shrewd of wit, prompt in quotation; but they prefer that their chief controversies with the world should be conducted by the spade.

Hence they thrive where no other men could live. Those engineers who reported that a hundred settlers could never find sustenance in these valleys, were not so much in the wrong as many people, wise after Young's success, suppose. Even Bridger, the old Wasatch trapper, when he offered to give a thousand dollars for every ear of corn to be raised in this valley, was not such a fool as his words may now seem to make him. Those critics only spoke of what might have been expected from ordinary men, impelled by ordinary motives; and nothing on earth is surer than that ordinary men would have perished in these regions. The soil is so dry, so barren, that with all his passion for work, a Mormon can only cultivate four acres of land, while a Gentile on the Missouri and the Kansas rivers can easily cultivate forty acres. Take away the Mormon impetus, and in two years this city of Salt Lake would come to depend, as Denver does, on Indiana and Ohio for its supplies of food.

Who, then, are these working Saints engaged in building this Temple?

Thirty-six years ago, there were six Mormons in America; none in England, none in the rest of Europe; and to-day (1866) they have twenty thousand Saints in Salt Lake City; four thousand each in Ogden, Provo, and Logan; in the whole of their stations in these valleys (one hundred and six settlements, properly organized by them, and ruled by bishops and elders), a hundred and fifty thousand souls; in other parts of the United States, about eight or ten thousand; in England and its dependencies, about fifteen thousand; in the rest of Europe, ten thousand; in Asia and the South Sea Islands, about twenty thousand; in all not less, perhaps, than two hundred thousand followers of the gospel preached by Joseph Smith. All these converts have been gathered into this Temple in thirty years.

This power of growth — a power developed in the midst of persecution — is one of the strangest facts in the story of this strange people. In half the span of our life they have risen from nothing into a vast and vital church. Islam, preaching the Unity of God with fire and sword, swept onward with a slower march than these American Saints; for in little more than thirty years they have won a nation from the Christian church; they have occupied a territory larger than Spain; they have built a capital in the desert, which is already more populous than Valladolid; they have drilled an army which I have reason to believe is more than twenty thousand strong; they have raised a priesthood, counting in its ranks many hundreds of working prophets, presidents, bishops, councillors, and elders; they have established a law, a theology, a social science, of their own, profoundly hostile to all reigning colleges and creeds.

Counting them man by man, the Saints are already strong; but the returns which are made on paper (so frequently beyond the mark in both churches and armies) stand in their case far below their actual strength, whether we weigh them in the scale of either temporal or spiritual power. Other men may be counted by heads; these men must be counted by heads and hearts; for every saint is at once a priest and a soldier; the whole Mormon population being trained alike to controversies of the spirit and of the flesh. Every male adult has a thought in his brain, a revolver in his belt, a rifle in his hand. In every house we find arms; in the Prophet's chamber, in the newspaper office, in the emigrants' shed, in the bath-house, in the common parlour, in the ordinary sleeping-room. On our first arrival at Salt Lake City, the hotel, kept by Colonel Little, a leading Mormon, was full of guests, and a small dog-hole, without a chair, a table, a wardrobe, and with only one camp-bed in it, was offered us by a hasty negro for our quarters. Letters of introduction, instantly delivered, brought friends to our help; but the place was so crammed with visitors that no room could be made or got, and my friend was obliged to accept Colonel Little's hospitalities at his private house. There he found one of the Colonel's wives reading to her group of pretty girls a book in favour of polygamy; and on being shown into a bed-room for the night (a bed-room belonging to one of Colonel Little's sons), he was startled on finding a loaded pistol under his pillow, two Colt's revolvers loaded and capped, slung on the wall; in a corner of the room two Ballard rifles. Young Little, whose room my friend was occupying for the night, is a lad of seventeen.

At first these Saints were a pacific race, warring with the sword of faith only; but when the Gentile spoiler came down upon them, using steel and lead against what they called truth, and when it appeared that the law, appealed to in their stress of mind and body, could give them no help, they girt upon their loins a more carnal weapon. They bought swords and guns, formed themselves into bands, fell steadily to drill, and in a few months they had become more formidable in Iowa and Illinois than their weak numbers could have made them. If they were not strong enough to found a new empire on the Mississippi in defiance of public opinion, they were powerful enough to disturb the adjoining States; and when the Mexican war broke out, to send a brilliant corps to the seat of war. From that day to our own, the martial exercises of the Saints have known no pause. Drill may now be considered as part of the Mormon ritual; a Saint being as much bound to appear on parade as he is in the tabernacle. It is scarcely a figure of speech to say that every male adult of Deseret — as the Mormons call Utah — holds himself equally ready to start on a mission and to take the field. It is their boast, and I believe not a vain one, that in fifteen minutes they can rally three thousand rifles, each rifle backed by a revolver, around their City hall. Once, on a false alarm being raised, this body of men was actually under arms.

These Temple builders call themselves Saints, accept the Bible as true, baptize their converts in the name of Christ; but they are not a Christian people, and no church in the world could hold communion with them in their present state. In truth, they approach much nearer both in creed, in morals, and in government, to the Utes and Shoshonees than to any Anglo-Saxon church. Young gets a meaning from the Bible which no one else ever found there. It has been often said that the Saints pretend to have a new translation of the Bible; a rendering made by the Holy Spirit; but Brigham Young tells me that this statement is untrue. He claims to understand the Scriptures by a purer light than we Gentiles now possess, and to have the hidden meaning of certain portions of them cleared by Divine revelation; but he takes our Bible as it stands in the authorized English version. "King James' Bible," he said to me with emphasis, "is my Bible; I know of none other." In fact, he seems to regard that version as in some sort divine, and the very language in which it is couched as in some sort sacred. "The English tongue," he said, "is a holy form of speech; the best, the softest, and the strongest language in the world." I think he considers it the language of God and of heaven. "It is holy," he said, "for it is the speech in which the angels wrote the Book of Mormon, the speech in which God has given his last revelation to man." When a friend of mine went into a Salt Lake City book-store, and asked for the Mormon book of faith, the man behind the counter handed him an English Bible. "We have no better book," he said; "all that we believe you will find in those pages." This is what they always say; but it is no less true that they find a thousand facts and doctrines in their Bible which we have never found in ours; a new history of the creation, of the fall, of the atonement, of the future life. In fact, they have made for themselves a new heaven and a new earth.

A Mohammedan mosque stands nearer to a Christian church than this Mormon temple stands. Islam broke down idols, Mormonism sets them up. Smith and Young have peopled their strange heaven with gods of their own making; and the Almighty is in their eyes but a President of Heaven, a Chief among spiritual peers, occupying a throne like that of the Roman Jove. In short, this temple is nothing less than the altar of a new people; a people having a new law, a new morality, a new priesthood, a new industry, a new canon, and a new God.

CHAPTER XIX.

The Two Seers.

Nothing is more easy than to laugh at these votaries. They are low people; scum of the earth, dregs of great cities, mire of the roadside, ooze of the river-bank and the ditch. Their prophet was Joe Smith; and that story of his about the gold plates, about the Urim and Thummim, about the Egyptian mummy, about the Spalding manuscript novel, about the Sword of Laban, and the angelic visitors, about the Mormon bank, the paper money, and the spiritual wife — may be so told by a man of comic vein as to excite shouts of laughter in a Gentile room. Perhaps the weakest side of the new church is that of the Prophet's actual life, as the strongest side is that of his actual death. Had Smith lived long enough for the facts of his career to become known, many persons think that among a people keenly alive to humour he would have found no lasting dupes.

Look, say these persons, into that oily, perky face, and say whether you can dream of anything divine lying hid behind it? Smith, having the true instinct of a sectarian, and knowing that the seeds of the Church were sown in the blood of her martyrs, put himself day by day into the paths of the persecutor. No man is popular until he has been abused, no man is thought a saint until he has been calumniated, no man is ranked among the prophets until he has been stoned to death. "Persecution," said Brigham, "is our portion; if we are right, the world will be against us; but the world will not prevail against the elect of God." Smith felt in his heart this truth of truths; he sought for oppression as the sign of his calling, and his enemies in the States indulged him in the dearest wish of his soul.

Thirty-nine times he was cited into courts of law. It is strong evidence of his craft that he contrived to be so often accused without being once condemned. Every charge made against him put new heart into his church. Still the growth of his sect was slow; slow, compared against that of George Fox, that of John Wesley, even that of Ann Lee. Round Smith's own person there was always bickering and division; many of the Saints declaring that their seer was robbing the common till. Rigdon, his partner in the fraud of palming off Spalding's romance as a translation from the golden plates, quitted and exposed him. Other men followed this example; and though many new converts were being made at a distance among people who knew not Joseph in the flesh, the sect could hardly have been kept together, had it not pleased the western rowdies to make Smith a martyr. A gang of ruffians, taking the law into their hands, broke into his prison at Carthage, and shot him down like a dog.

A crime, for which no excuse could be found, infused new spirit into his friends, and opened to his missionaries the ears of thousands. After the murder had been committed, justice was too slow to seize, too weak to punish his assassins; a fact which seemed to carry the appeal of blood from earth to heaven.

When it became known that Smith was dead — that he had been slain for his opinions — his faults were instantly swept aside; the remembrance of his craft, his greed, his sensuality, his ignorance, his ambition, was buried in his secret grave; and the unsought glory of a martyr's death was counted to him by his people, and by many who had not till then become his people, as of higher virtue than would have been the merit of a saintly and heroic life.

It is a story as old as time. Smith — living at Nauvoo, squabbling with his apostles about debts and duns, wrangling with his wife Emma about spiritual wives, subject to constant accusations of theft and drunkenness — was certainly not a man whom the American people had any cause to fear; but his assassination in the gaol at Carthage raised this alleged debtor and drunkard, this alleged thief and fornicator, into the rank of a saint. Men who could hardly have endured his presence in the flesh proclaimed him, now that he was gone, as a true successor of Moses and of Christ.

Under a new leader, Brigham Young — a man of lowly birth, of keen humour, of unerring good sense — the sect emerged from its condition of internal strife; putting on a more decent garb, closing up its broken ranks, labouring with a new zeal, extending its missionary work. Finding that through recent troubles his position on the Mississippi had become untenable, Young advised his followers to yield their prize, to quit the world in which they had found no peace, and set up their tabernacles in one of those distant wilds in the far West, which were then trodden by no feet of men, except those of a few Red Indian tribes, Utes, Pawnees, Shoshonees, in what was called the American desert, and was considered by everybody as No-man's land. It was a bold device. Beyond the western prairies, beyond the Rocky Mountains, lay a howling wilderness of salt and stones, a property which no white man had yet been greedy enough to claim. Some pope, in the middle ages, had bestowed it on the crown of Spain, from which it had fallen, as a paper waste, to the Mexican Republic; but neither Spaniard nor Mexican had ever gone up north into the land to possess it. In the centre of this howling wilderness lay a Dead Sea, not less terrible than Bahr Lout, the Sea of Lot. One-fourth of its water was known to be solid salt. The creeks which run into it were said to be putrid; the wells around it were known to be bitter; and the shores for many miles were crusted white with saleratus. These shores were like nothing else on earth, except the Syrian Ghor, and they were more forbidding than the Syrian Ghor in this particular, that the waters of Salt Lake are dull, impure, and the water lines studded with ditches and pools intolerable to the nostrils of living men. To crown its repulsive features, this desert of salt, of stones, and of putrid creeks, was shut off from the world, eastward by the Rocky Mountains, westward by the Sierra Nevada, ranges of alps high as the chain of Mont Blanc, and covered with eternal ice and snow.

The red men who roamed over this country in search of roots and insects, were known to be the most savage and degraded tribes of their savage and degraded race. A herd of bison, a flight of gulls, a swarm of locusts, peopled the plain with a fitful life. In spring, when a little verdure rose upon the ground, a little wild sage, a few dwarf sun-flowers, the locusts sprang from the earth and stript the few green plants of every leaf and twig. No forests could be seen; the grass, where it grew, appeared to be rank and thin. Only the wild sage and the dwarf sun-flower seemed to find food in the soil, plants which are useless to man, and were then thought to be poisonous to his beast.

Trappers, who had looked down on the Salt Valley from peaks and passes in the Wasatch Mountains, pictured it as a region without life, without a green slope, even without streams and springs. The wells were said to be salt, as the fields were salt. Finding no wood, and scarcely any fresh water in that region, these explorers had set their seal upon this great American desert as a waste unfit for the dwelling, incapable of the sustenance, of civilised men. But Young thought otherwise. He knew that where the Saint had struck his spade into the ground — at Kirtland in Ohio, at Independence in Missouri, at Nauvoo in Illinois — he had been always blessed with a plentiful crop; and the new Mormon seer had faith in the same strong sinews, in the same rough hands, in the same keen will, being able to draw harvests of grain from the desolate valley of Salt Lake.

A carpenter by trade, Young knew how to fell trees, to shape logs, to build carts and trucks, to stake out ground, to erect temporary sheds. The Saints whom he would have to lead were inured to labour and privation; being chiefly New England artisans and Western farmers, men who could turn their hands to any trade, who could face any difficulty, execute any work. An equal number of either English or French converts would have perished in the attempt to move across the plains and the mountains; but the native American is a man of all trades — a banker, a butcher, a carpenter, a clerk, a teamster, a statesman, anything at a pinch, everything in its turn — a man rich in resources and ingenuities, so that a baker can build you a bridge, a preacher can catch you a wild horse, a lawyer can bake you hot cakes. Young knew that in crossing the great plains and in climbing the great ranges, which are loosely clubbed together under the name of Rocky Mountains, the privations of his people would be sharp; but to his practical eye these sufferings of the flesh appeared to be such as brave men could be trained by example to bear and not die. Food and seed might be carried in their light waggons, and a little malt whisky would correct the alkali in the bitter creeks. In his band of disciples every man was master of some craft; every woman was either a dairy-maid, a baker, a seamstress, a laundress; nay, the children could be turned to account in the desert roads, for every American girl can milk a cow, every American boy can drive a team.

A party of pioneers (many of whom are still alive in Salt Lake Valley) having been sent forward to explore and report, the word to move on westward was at length given by Young, and in every family of Nauvoo preparations were made for a journey, unmatched in history since the days when Moses led the Israelites out of Egypt. The Saints broke up their cheery homes. They gathered, in their haste, a little food, a few roots and seeds, a dozen kegs of spirits. Then they yoked their mules, their oxen, to the country waggons. Those who were too poor to buy waggons and oxen, made for themselves trucks and wheel-barrows. Pressed upon by their foes, they marched away from Nauvoo, even while the winter was yet hard upon them, crossing the Mississippi on the ice, and starting on a journey of fifteen hundred miles, through a country without a road, without a bridge, without a village, without an inn, without wells, cattle, pastures, and cultivated land. As Elder John Taylor told me, they left everything behind; their corn-fields, their gardens, their pretty houses, with the books, carpets, pianos, everything which they contained. The distance to be conquered by these emigrants was equal to that from London to Lemberg, six times that from Cairo to Jerusalem. Their route lay through a prairie peopled by Pawnees, Shoshonees, wolves and bears; it was broken by rapid rivers, barred by a series of mountain chains; and the haven to be reached, after all their toils and dangers, was the shore of a Dead Sea, lying in a sterile valley; a land watered with brine, and pastures sown with salt.

CHAPTER XX.

Flight from Bondage.

THE tale of that journey of the Saints, as we hear it from the lips of Young, of Wells, of Taylor, and of other old men who made it, is a story to wring and yet nerve the hearts of all generous men. When these Mormons were driven by violence from the roofs which they had built, the fields which they had tilled, the days were short and snow lay thick upon the ground. Everything, save a little food for the way-side, a few corn-seeds and potato-roots for the coming year, had to be abandoned to their armed and riotous enemies; the homes which they had made, the temple they had just finished, the graves they had recently dug. Frost bit their little ones in the hands and feet. Hunger and thirst tormented both young and aged. Long plains of sand, into which the waggon-wheels sank to the axle-trees, separated the scanty supplies of water. Wells there were none. Mirage often mocked them with its promise; and even when they came to creeks and streams they often found them bitter to the taste, and dangerous to health. The days were short and cold, and the absence of any other shelter from the frost than the bit of canvas roof made the nights of winter terrible to all. Horses sickened by the way. Disease broke out among the cows and sheep, so that milk ran short, and the supplies of mutton were dressed and cooked in fear. Some of the poor, the aged, and the ailing, had then to be left behind; with them a guard of young men who could ill be spared.

Nor was this loss of a part of their youth and strength the whole of their calamity in this opening stage of their emigration. Just at the hour when every male arm was most precious to these exiles, the Mexican war broke out; and a government, which had never been strong enough to do them right, came down to them for help in arms and men. Young answered the appeal of his country like a patriot: five hundred youths, the flower of his migrating bands, stepped out before him, and with the blessing of their chief upon their heads, they mustered themselves into the invading corps.

Weakened by the departure of this living force, the Mormons crossed the Missouri River in a ferry made by themselves, entering on the great wilderness, the features of which they laid down on a map,. making a rough road, and throwing light bridges over streams, as they went on; collecting grass and herbs for their own use; sowing corn for those who were to come later in the year; raising temporary sheds in which their little ones might sleep; and digging caves in the earth as a refuge from the winter snow. Their food was scarce, their water bad, and such wild game as they could find in the plains, the elk, the antelope, the buffalo, poisoned their blood. Nearly all the malt whisky which they had brought from Nauvoo to correct the bad water, had been seized on the road, and the kegs staved in, by agents of government, on pretence of its being meant for the red-skins, to whom it was unlawful for the whites to sell any ardent spirits. Four kegs only had been saved: saved by Brigham Young himself. An elder, who was present in the boat, and who told me the anecdote, says it is the only time he ever remembers to have seen the Prophet in a rage. Four kegs were on board the ferry, when the officer seized them and began to knock in the staves; in that spirit lay the lives of the people; and when Brigham saw the man raise his mallet, he drew his pistol, levelled it at his head, and cried, "Stay your hand! If you touch that keg, you die by the living God!" The man jumped off the ferry and troubled them no more.

In our own journey across the plains, though the time was August, the weather fine, the passage swift, we suffered keenly from the want of fresh food and of good water. My companion sickened from bile into dysentery; no meat, no drink, would lie in his stomach; nothing but the cognac in our flasks. The water almost killed him. His sunburnt face grew chalky-white; his limbs hung feeble and relaxed; his strong physique so drooped that a man at one of the ranches, after looking at him for a moment with a curious eye, came up to me, and said, "You will feel very lonely when he is left behind." My own attack came later, and in another form. The skin of my hands peeled off, as if it had been either frayed or scraped with a knife; boils came out upon my back; a pock started on my under eye-lid; my fingers had the appearance of scorbutic eruptions.

FLIGHT FROM BONDAGE. 193

These two diseases, Taylor told me, ravaged the camp of emigrants. Many sickened of dysentery, still more suffered from scurvy.

Some of the Saints fell back in the face of these terrible trials. More fainted by the way-side, and were mournfully laid in their desert graves. Every day there came a funeral, every night there was fresh mourning in the camp. The waste of life is always very great in the emigrant trains; even now, when the roads are made and the stations are provisioned with vegetable food. Of the train which I saw come in, six had perished on the plains. A young lady told me that eighty had died in the train by which she had arrived; forty would perhaps be an average loss in the mountains and the plains. But no subsequent train has ever suffered like the first. "The waste of life was great," said Brigham Young, as he told me the dreadful tale. Yet the brave, unbroken body of male and female Saints toiled along the frozen way. When their hearts were very low, a band of music struck up some lively air, in which the people joined, and forgot their woes. By day they sang hymns, at night they danced round the watch-fires. Gloom, asperity, asceticism, they banished from their camps and from their thoughts. Among the few treasures which they had carried with them from Nauvoo was a printing-press; and a sheet of news, printed and published by the way-side, carried words of good counsel into every part of the camp.

After crossing the sands and creeks which have since become known to civilised men on maps and charts as Nebraska and Dakota, they arrived at the foot of the first great range of those high and broken chains of alps which are commonly grouped together under the name of Rocky Mountains; over these high barriers there was yet no path; and the defiles leading through them were buried in drifts of snow. How the Saints toiled up those mountain-sides, dragging with them oxen and carts, foraging for food, baking their bread and cooking their meat, without help and without guides, it brings tears into the eyes of aged men to tell. The young and bold went forward in advance; driving away the bears and wolves; stoning the rattle-snakes; chasing the elk and the wild deer; making a path for the women and the old men. At length, when they had reached the summit of the pass, they gazed upon a series of arid and leafless plains, of dry river-beds, of verdureless hillsides, of alkaline bottoms; pools of bitter water, narrow canyons and gorges, abrupt and steep. Day by day, week after week, they toiled over these bleak sierras, through these forbidding valleys. Food was running out; wild game became scarce; the Utes and Snakes were unfriendly; and at the end of their journey, should they ever reach it, lay the dry Salt desert, in which they had consented to come and dwell!

Yet they were not disheartened by these hostile aspects of the country; they had not expected a verdant paradise; they knew that the land had never been seized, because it had not been considered worth taking from the Indian tribes; they expected to find here nothing beyond peace and freedom, a place in which they could take their chance with Nature, and to which they could invite the Saints, their brethren, to a country of their own. Descending the passes with beating hearts and clanging trumpets, they entered on their lonely inheritance; marched upon this slope above the Jordan, near the conical hill on which Brigham had seen the angel in his sleep; laid down the plan of a new city; explored the canyons and water-courses into the hills; and in a few days found, to their sudden joy, not only springs of fresh water, but woody nooks and grassy mounds and slopes.

Not an hour was lost. "The first duty of a Saint when he comes to this valley," said Brigham Young to me, "is to learn how to grow a vegetable; after which he must learn how to rear pigs and fowls, to irrigate his land, and to build up his house. The rest will come in time." Ruled from the first by this practical genius, every man fell to his work. Deseret — country of the Bee — was announced as the Promised Land and future home of the Saints. It was to them as an unknown, unappropriated soil, and they hoped to found upon it an independent State.

CHAPTER XXI.

Settlement in Utah.

Soon the aspects of this desert valley began to change under their cunning hands; creeks from the hills being coaxed into new paths; fields being cleared and sown; homesteads rising from the ground; sheep and cattle beginning to dot the hills; salt-pits and saw-mills being established; fruit trees being planted and orchards taught to bloom and bear. Roads were laid out and made. When the Mormon herdsmen entered the hill ravines, they found pine and cotton-wood, elder, birch, and box; materials precious for the building of their new homes. A new Jerusalem sprang from the ground; a temple was commenced; a newspaper was published. Walnut and other hard woods were planted in favourable spots. The red-skins, who had long been the dread of all scouts and trappers in the far west, were won by courtesies and gifts; and in a few months they appeared to have been changed from enemies of the white men into allies. "We found it cheaper," said Colonel Little, "to feed the Indians than to fight them;" and this policy of feeding the Utes and Snakes has been pursued by Young, with two or three brief intervals of misunderstanding, from the day of his first settlement in the valley. For two or three trying years, the Saints of Salt Lake had to wage war against locusts and crickets, those plagues of the older Canaan; but by help of gulls from the lakes, and of their own devices in trapping and pounding the insects, the Mormons contrived to preserve their crops of corn and fruit. A year went by, and the Mormons had not perished in the waste. On the contrary, they had begun to grow, and even to make money. Year after year they have increased in numbers and in wealth, until their merchants are known in London and New York, and their city has become a wonder of the earth.

What are the secrets of this surprising growth of the new society out in these western deserts?

"Look around you," said Young to me, "if you want to know what kind of people we are. Nineteen years ago this valley was a desert, growing nothing but the wild sage and the dwarf sun-flower; we who came into it brought nothing with us but a few oxen and waggons, and a bag of seeds and roots; the people who came after us, many of them weavers and artisans, brought nothing, not a cent, not even skill and usage of the soil; and when you look from this balcony you can see what we have made of it."

How, above all other settlers in the waste lands of western America, have the Saints achieved this work?

Is it an answer to say that these Saints are dupes and fanatics? Nothing is easier than to laugh at Joe Smith and his church; but what then? The great facts remain. Young and his people are at Utah; a church of two hundred thousand souls; an army of twenty thousand rifles. You may smile at

Joseph's gift of tongues; his discovery of Urim and Thummim (which he supposed to have been a pair of spectacles!); his Sword of Laban; his prose works of Abraham; his Egyptian papyrus; his Mormon paper money; his thirty-nine trials. You may prove, with a swift and biting irony, that the weakest side of this new faith is the actual life of its founder; but will your wit disperse this camp of fanatics? Will your laughter shake down the walls of this New Jerusalem? Will your irony change the Utes and Shoshonees into enemies of these Saints? Will your arguments arrest those bands of missionaries which are employed in preaching, in a hundred places and to thousands of willing ears, the gospel as it was in Joseph? The hour has gone by, as Americans feel, for treating this Church in sport.

In England, though our soil is said to be the nursery of the Saints, we have not yet learned to think of Mormonism otherwise than as one of our many humours; as a rash that comes out from time to time in our social body; a sign, perhaps, of our occasional lack of health; no one among us has learned to regard it as the symptom of a disease which may be lying at the seat of life. Has Convocation ever given up a day to the Book of Mormon? Has a bishop ever visited the Saints in Commercial Road? Two or three ministers may have fired off pamphlets against them; but have any of these reverend fathers been to see them in their London homes? Rare, indeed, has been this holy strife even on the part of private men. But our brethren in America can hardly affect to treat the

Saints in this easy style. The new Church is visible among them; for good and evil it is in their system; not a humour to be cast out like a rash upon the skin. Up to this time our own Saints have been taught to regard England as Egypt, and their old dwelling-place as exile from a brighter home. America is to them Canaan, Salt Lake City a New Jerusalem. I do not say that this is good for us, though it has an appearance of being good, since it relieves us of a painful duty, and removes from the midst of our cities a cause of shame. The poor, the aged, the feeble, among the Saints, may be left behind in our streets, to die, as they think and say, in the house of bondage; but the rich, the young, the zealous, are bound by their faith to go forward and possess themselves of the Promised Land. With the younger Saints, especially with the female Saints, a change of air is always recommended on a change of creed. Thousands emigrate, though it is also true that thousands remain behind. In London, Liverpool, Glasgow, and in other cities, the Saints have schools and chapels, books and journals, of which Oxford knows little, and Mayfair less. Not being a political sect, never asking for any right, never urging any wrong; content with doing their work in peace; they escape notice from the press, and engage the thoughts of society as little as the Moravians and the Plymouth Brethren. In London society you may hear in any one week more speculation about Prince and Home, the Abode of Love and the Spiritual Spheres, than you will hear about Young and Deseret in six months. The

Saints are not in society; but in Boston, Washington, and New York, these Mormons are a fearful portent, threatening to become a formidable power. Already they have put jurists into session and armies into motion. Colfax, the Speaker, has been to confer with Young; and committees of Congress are sitting on the affairs of Utah. The day appears to be drawing nigh when the problems which these Mormons put before the world may have to be considered by practical men, not in colleges and chapels only, not in senates and in courts of law only, but in the camp and in the battle-field.

That question of how these Mormons are to be dealt with by the American people, is one of the strangest riddles of an age which has bridged the ocean, put a girdle of lightnings round the earth, and tamed to its service the fiery steeds of the sun. A true reply may be far to seek; for we have not yet resolved, finally, how far thought is free from the control of law; and to what extent toleration of creeds implies toleration of the conduct which springs from creeds. One step in advance towards such a reply must be an attempt to find what Mormonism is, and by what means it has grown. It cannot be put aside as either unmixed foolishness or unalloyed vice. Strange as the new sectarians may seem to us, they must have in their keeping some grain of truth. They live and thrive, and men who live by their own labour, thrive by their own enterprise, cannot be altogether mad. Their streets are clean, their houses bright, their gardens fruitful. Peace reigns in their cities. Harlots and drunkards are unknown among them,

They keep open more common schools than any other sect in the United States. But being what they are, believing what they do, their merits are perhaps more trying to our patience than their crimes. It is thought that many persons in the United States would be able to endure them a little better if they would only behave themselves a good deal worse.

What have these Saints achieved?

In the midst of a free people, they have founded a despotic power. In a land which repudiates state religions, they have placed their church above human laws. Among a society of Anglo-Saxons, they have introduced some of the ideas, many of the practices, of Red Indian tribes, of the Utes, Shoshonees, and Snakes. In the nineteenth century after Christ, they have revived the social habits which were common in Syria nineteen hundred years before His birth.

Hints for their system of government may have been found nearer home than Hauran, in less respectable quarters than the Bible. The Shoshonee wigwam could have supplied the Saints with a nearer model of a plural household than the Patriarch's tent; but this fact, if it were true, would hardly be confessed by Kimball and Young. As they state their case, Abraham is their perfect man; who forsook his home, his kindred, and his country, for the sake of God. Sarai is their perfect woman; because she called her husband lord, and gave her handmaid Hagar into his bosom for a wife. Everything that Abraham did, they pronounce it right for them to do; all gospels and commandments of the

Church, all laws and institutes of man, being void and of no effect when quoted against the practices of that Arab sheikh. Putting under their feet both the laws of science and the lessons of history, they preach the duty of going back, in the spirit and in the name, to that priestly and paternal form of government which existed in Syria four thousand years ago; casting from them, as so much waste, the things which all other white men have learned to regard as the most precious conquests of time and thought — personal freedom, family life, change of rulers, right of speech, concurrence in laws, equality before the judge, liberty of writing and voting. They cast aside these conquests of time and thought in favour of Asiatic obedience to a man without birth, without education, whom they have chosen to regard as God's own vicar on the earth. No Pope in Rome, no Czar in Moscow, no Caliph in Bagdad, ever exercised such power as the Mormons have conferred on Young. "I am one of those men," said to me Elder Stenhouse — perhaps the man of highest culture whom we saw at Salt Lake City — "who think that Brother Brigham ought to do everything; he has made this church, and he ought to have his way in everything." Many others said the same thing, in nearly the same words. No one would dispute Young's will. "A man had better go to hell at once," said Stenhouse, "if he cannot meet Brigham's eye." In a caste of Hindoos, in a family of Kirghis, in a tribe of Bedaween, such an act of prostration would have seemed to me strange; in free America, among the countrymen of Sydney and

Washington, coming from the lips of a writer who could make jokes and quote the last poem, and who is enough American to carry two revolvers in his pockets, it was more than strange. It was a sign.

CHAPTER XXII.

Work and Faith.

Joseph Smith, a poor lad, born in Sharon, Windsor County, Vermont, the son of unlettered parents, had been crazed by one of those revivals which Elder Frederick, the Shaker preacher at Mount Lebanon, regards as the providential season of religious life. This untaught boy had begun to work upon the passions which he felt in play around him; announcing, like many others, but with more insistence than his fellows, that in his trances of body he had received angelic visitors, that he had spoken with God face to face, that he had been chosen to plant a new Church on earth; a Church of America, the new Canaan, chosen from the beginnings of time to be the home of a new creed and the seat of a new empire. Men who had come to hear him had gone away converted; he had told them that a new priesthood had been chosen, that God had planted his kingdom once again; they had left him convinced, and gone away from his presence carrying these glad tidings into thousands of Christian homes. No force had been used, none could have been used in that early stage of their career; for the Saints had then no weapon save the word; they toiled in a pacific vineyard, and made their conquests in the face of vigilant foes. A fair hearing for their gospel, an open field for their preachers, were all they had asked, and more than what they had received. They sent no Khaled to the nations, with his offer of either conversion, slavery, or death; not because such a line of policy would have been contrary to the genius of their creed; but simply because, in a free state, and under a secular law, they had found no means for carrying out their plans. From the day of their dawn an Arab spirit had been strong upon them. Should a time ever come when they can cut their withes and buckle on their swords, they may be found fierce as Gideon, ruthless as Omar; but in the past they have been obliged to occupy the ground of a suffering rather than that of a militant Church. Everything done by them as yet has been effected by word of mouth, by what they describe as the power of truth.

How have these settlers in the wilderness done the things we see?

Simply, answers Young, by the power of work and faith; by doing what they profess, by believing what they say.

Nearly all the forces which are found most powerful to sway men's minds in our lay societies, — genius, reputation, office, birth, and riches, — have being wanting to these Saints. No man of the stamp of Luther, Calvin, Wesley, has appeared among them. In intellect, Joseph was below contempt. Brigham is a man of keen good sense. Pratt is a dreamer. Kimball is unlettered. Wells, Cannon, Taylor, Hooper, — the brightest men among them, — have shown no worldly gifts, no scholarship, eloquence, poetry, and logic, to account for such sudden and sustained success as they have met with in every land.

The bee has been chosen by the Saints as an emblem of Deseret, though Nature has all but denied that insect to this dry and flowerless land. Young's house is called the Beehive; in it no drone ever finds a place; for the Prophet's wives are bound to support themselves by needle-craft, teaching, spinning, dyeing yarn, and preserving fruit. Every woman in Salt Lake has her portion of work, each according to her gifts, every one steadfastly believing that labour is noble and holy; a sacrifice meet for man to make, and for God to accept. Ladies make gloves and fans, dry peaches and figs, cut patterns, prepare seeds, weave linen, and knit hose. Lucy and Emiline, sometimes called the lights of Brigham's harem, are said to be prodigies of skill in the embroidery of flowers. Some of Emiline's needlework is certainly fine, and Susan's potted peaches are beyond compare. On men fall the heavier toils of the field, the ditch, and the hill-side, where they break the ground, dam up the river, fell the maple and the dwarf-oak, pasture the cattle, and catch the wild horse. But the sexes take each their share of a common task: rearing houses, planting gardens, starting workshops, digging mines: each with a strain of energy and passion never found on the eastern slopes of this Wasatch chain.

The ministry is unprofessional and unpaid. Every

Saint being a priest, no man in the church is suffered to accept a cent for his service, even though his time, his faculties, his life itself, should be spent in doing what his brethren regard as the work of God. Duty to the church comes first; duty to the family, to the individual, comes next; but with such an interval as puts collision and confusion utterly out of question.

Prophets, presidents, bishops, elders, all pursue their avocations in the city and on the soil; sell ribbons, grow peaches, build mills, cut timber, keep ranches, herd cattle, drive trains. One day, we met a venerable man, with a small basket on his arm, covered with a snow-white napkin; his appearance struck us; and we learned that he was Joseph Young, elder brother of Brigham, and President of the Seventy. He was taking his basket of peaches to market for sale.

An apostle holds the plough, a patriarch drives a team. In a city where work is considered holy, the brightest dignitary gains in popular repute by engaging in labour and in trade. These Saints have not one idle gentleman in their church. Brigham Young is a mill-owner, cotton-planter, farmer; Heber Kimball is a mill-owner, grazier, manufacturer of linseed oil; George Smith is a farmer and miller; Orson Pratt is a teacher of mathematics; Orson Hyde is a farmer; John Taylor, formerly a wood-turner, is now a mill-owner; Wilford Woodruff is a farmer and grazier; George Cannon is a printer and editor. These men are the foremost lights in the church, and they are all men of laborious, secular habits. Young, Kimball, Taylor, are now rich men; the twelve apostles are said to be mostly poor; but, whether they are rich or poor, these Mormon elders live on what they can earn by the labour of their hands and brains, taking nothing, it is said, for their loftier services in the church.

The unpaid functions of a bishop are extremely numerous; for a Mormon prelate has to look, not merely to the spiritual welfare of his flock, but to their worldly interest and well-being; to see that their farms are cultivated, their houses clean, their children taught, their cattle lodged. Last Sunday, after service at the Tabernacle, Brigham Young sent for us to the raised dais on which he and the dignitaries had been seated, to see a private meeting of the bishops, and to hear what kind of work these reverend fathers had met to do. We rather wondered what our friends at Bishopsthorpe and Wells would think of such a scene. The old men gathered in a ring; and Edward Hunter, their presiding bishop, questioned each and all as to the work going on in his ward, the building, painting, draining, gardening; also as to what this man needed, and that man needed, in the way of help. An emigrant train had just come in, and the bishops had to put six hundred persons in the way of growing their cabbages and building their homes. One bishop said he could take five bricklayers, another two carpenters, a third a tinman, a fourth seven or eight farm-servants, and so on through the whole bench. In a few minutes I saw that two hundred of these poor emigrants had been placed in the way of earning their daily bread. "This," said Young, with a sly little smile, "is one of the labours of our bishops." I confess, I could not see much harm in it.

———

CHAPTER XXIII.

Missionary Labour.

The spirit of the Mormon church may best be read in the missionary labours of these Saints. It is their boast, that when they go out to convert the Gentiles, they carry with them no purse, no scrip; that they go forth, naked and alone, to do the Lord's work in the Lord's way; trusting in no arm of flesh, in no power of gold; taking no thought of what they shall eat and where they shall lie down; but putting their lives and fortunes wholly into the hands of God.

The way in which an elder may be called to such missionary work has, in this age of dollars, an air of primitive romance. Young (say) is walking down Main Street; he sees a young fellow driving a team, galloping a horse, riding in a cart; a thought comes into his prophetic mind; and, calling that young elder to his side, he tells him that the Lord has chosen him to go forth and preach, mentioning, perhaps, the period and the place; the time may be for one year, for three years, for ten years; the locality may be in Liverpool, in Damascus, in Delhi, in Pekin. Asking only a few hours' time to put his house in order, to take leave of his friends, to kiss his wives and children, that young elder, chosen from the street, will start on his errand of grace.

I have talked with a dozen of such missionaries; young men who have been called from the ranch, from the saw-mill, from the peach-garden, at a moment's notice, to depart without purse or scrip, to go forth, naked and alone, into the ends of the earth. Elder Stenhouse had been sent to labour in France and Switzerland, Elder Riter in Austria, Elder Naisbit in England, Elder Dewey in India and Ceylon. Their method was the same.

Without money and without food, the missionary starts on his journey; hiring himself as a driver, a guard, a carpenter, to some train of merchandise going either towards the river or towards the sea, as the case may be. If his sphere is Europe, the young elder works as a labourer to New York, where he hires himself out either as a clerk, or as a mechanic, according to his gifts, until he can save his passage-money; if this course is inconvenient to him, either as to his person or his mission, he agrees with some skipper to serve before the mast, on which he will take his place humbly with the poor sailors, to whom, as the ship heaves onward, he finds many opportunities for preaching the glad tidings of a Mormon's rest in the Valley of the Mountains. He is not a man of books. "We have no colleges here," said Young, "to train our young men to be fools; we just take a fellow from the hills, who has been felling wood, killing bears and catching wild colts; we send him out on a mission, and he comes back to us a man." Arrived in Europe, without a penny, without a home, the missionary finds, if he can, a lodging in the house of some local saint. If he cannot find such lodging, he sleeps on a bench, on a stone step, under a tree, among the litter of a dock. "I landed in Southampton," said Elder Stenhouse, when relating his many victories of the spirit, "without a farthing in my purse, and I sold the boots from my feet to buy a plank from which I could preach." Elder Dewey told me he had travelled from Salt Lake to San Francisco, from San Francisco to Ceylon, from Ceylon to Poonah, toiling, preaching, begging, never fearing for the flesh, but confiding everywhere and always in the protection of God; labouring among Californian miners, among Chinese sailors, among Cingalese farmers, among Bombay teamsters and muleteers, seldom wanting for a shelter, never wanting for a meal. Such is the spirit of the young Mormon elder. Sometimes he is helped forward by a Saint, oftentimes by a stranger and a Gentile; at the worst, he gets employment as a tailor, as a carpenter, as a dockyard labourer. Living on crusts of bread, sleeping beneath lowly roofs, he toils and preaches from town to town, ardent in the doing of his daily task; patient, abstinent, obscure; courting no notice, rousing no debates; living the poor man's life; offering himself everywhere as the poor man's friend. When his task is done, he will preach his way back from the scene of his labour to his pleasant home, to his thriving farm, to his busy mill, in the valley of the Great Salt Lake.

In this Mormon city, where every man is an elder, almost every man is a priest. Any Saint, therefore, may be called to these missionary toils;

and no Eastern slave obeys his master with such swift alacrity as that which is shown by the Saint who is called by Young to start for a distant land.

The glad tidings which men like Dewey and Stenhouse scatter among deck-passengers, dockmen, street-porters, farm-servants, and their fellows, are of a kind which the desolate and the discontented long to hear. They pronounce against the world and the world's ways. They declare the need for a great change; they promise the poor man merrier times and a brighter home. They offer the starving bread, the houseless roofs, the naked clothes. To the craftsman they promise mills, to the peasant farms. The heaven of which they tell is not placed by them wholly beyond the grave; earth itself is, in their opinion, a part of heaven; and as the earth and all that is in it are the Lord's, they announce that these riches of the earth are the true inheritance of His saints. The rich, they say, have corrupted the faith of Christ, and the churches of the rich are engaged in the devil's work. They represent Joseph as a pastor of the poor. They suggest that ignorance is a saving virtue, and that lowly people are the favourites of God.

Other churches besides that of the Saints hold some of these gospels; but the Mormon preacher is seen to act as though he believed them to be true. Show the young missionary a beggar, an outcast, a thief, — one who is in despair and ready to perish, — and he will act as though he considered himself chosen of God to save that miserable wretch. With men who appear in fine clothes, who dwell in great houses, who dine off silver plate, he has no concern. His task lies in Five Points, not in Madison Square; in Seven Dials, not in Park Lane. The rich, the learned, the polite, have their own creeds and rituals, beyond his power to either mend or mar. They have no need of him, and he never seeks them in their pride. What could he say to them? Would they listen to his promise of a brighter day? Would they care for his paradise of farms and pastures? Passing these worldlings by, as men to whom he has not been sent, the Saint goes lower in the scale of life; seeking out those victims of the world for whom no one but himself appears to care. In the wants and cravings of the poor he finds an opening for his message. But he does not praise the lowly for being poor; he does not lead them to infer that a state of pauperism is a state of grace; his doctrine is, that riches are good things; and he holds out a promise, which he can back by a thousand examples, that the Saints will become rich by the toil of their hands and by the blessing of God. To men hungering after lands and houses, the prosperity which he can truly describe as existing in Deseret, and which he warmly invites them to come and share, is a great and potential fact.

Care of the poor is written down strongly in the Mormon code of sacred duties. A bishop's main function is to see that no man in his ward, in his county, is in want of food and raiment; when he finds that a poor family is in need, he goes to his more prosperous neighbour, and in the Lord's name demands from him a sack of wheat, a can of tea, a loaf of sugar, a blanket, a bed; knowing that his requisition will be promptly met. The whole earth is the Lord's, and must be rendered up to Him. Elder Jennings, the richest merchant in Salt Lake City, told me of many such requisitions being made upon himself; in bad times, they may come upon him twice or thrice a-day. In case of need, the bishop goes up to the Tithing office and obtains the succour of which his parishioner stands in need; for the wants of the poor take precedence of the wants of the church; but the appeal from personal benevolence to the public fund has seldom to be made. For if a Saint has any kind of store, he must share it with his fellow; if he has bread, he must feed the hungry; if he has raiment, he must clothe the naked. No excuse avails him for neglect of this great duty. The command to sell what we have and give the money to the poor, is to most of us an empty rule; but the Mormon, like the Arab and the Jew, whose spirit he has had breathed into him, knows nothing of such pious fictions. "Feed my flock," is to him an injunction that admits of no denial, and of no delay.

A special fund is raised for the relief of necessitous Saints; and Young himself, the servant of all, discharges in person the troublesome duties of this trust. I went with Bishop Hunter, a good and merry old man, full of work and humour, to the emigrants' corral, to see the rank and file of the new English arrivals; six hundred people from the Welsh hills and from the Midland shires; men, women, and children; all poor and uncomely, weary, dirty, freckled with the sun, scorbutic from privation; when I was struck by the tender tones of his voice, the wisdom of his counsel, the fatherly solicitude of his manner in dealing with these poor people. Some of the women were ill and querulous; they wanted butter, they wanted tea; they wanted many things not to be got in the corral. Hunter sent for a doctor from the city, and gave orders for tea and butter on the Tithing office. Never shall I forget the yearning thankfulness of expression which beamed from some of these sufferers' eyes. The poor creatures felt that in this aged bishop they had found a wise and watchful friend.

Yet the Saints, as a rule, are not poor in the sense in which the Irish are poor; not needy as a race, a body, and a church; indeed, for a new society, starting with nothing, and having its fortunes to make by labour, they are rich. Utah is sprinkled with farms and gardens; the hill-sides are pictured with flocks and herds; and the capital city, the New Jerusalem, is finely laid out and nobly built. Every man labours with his hand and brain; the people are frugal; their fields cost them nothing; and the wealth created by their industry is great. To multiply flocks and herds, to lay up corn and wheat, is with them to obey the commands of God.

CHAPTER XXIV.

Mormon Light.

FULLY to comprehend these Saints, you must look beyond the beauty of their city, the prosperity of their farms, the activity of their workshops, the extent of their villages, into the spiritual sources of their strength.

Joseph taught his disciples a doctrine by no means new; that in every religion there is a germ of good, and perhaps a germ of evil; and he proposed by divine assistance (and the aid of Rigdon, Young, and Pratt) to extract the grain of good out of every old creed, and add it to the church which he was founding for his people. He took much from Mohammed, more from Paul, most of all from Abraham; but in his free handling of religious notions, he had no scruple about borrowing from the Hindoos, from the Tartars, from the Mohawks. The doctrinal notes of his church may be numbered and explained: —

1. God is a person, with the form and flesh of man.

2. Man is a part of the substance of God, and will himself become a god.

3. Man was not created by God, but existed from all eternity, and will exist to all eternity.

4. Man is not born in sin, and is not accountable for offences other than his own.

5. The earth is a colony of embodied spirits, one of many such settlements in space.

6. God is President of the Immortals, having under him four orders of beings: (1), Gods — that is to say, immortal beings, possessed of a perfect organisation of soul and body; being the final state of men who have lived on earth in perfect obedience to the law: (2), Angels — immortal beings, who have lived on earth in imperfect obedience to the law: (3), Men — immortal beings, in whom a living soul is united with a human body: (4), Spirits — immortal beings, still waiting to receive their tabernacle of flesh.

7. Man, being one of the race of gods, becomes eligible, by means of marriage, for a celestial throne; his household of wives and children being his kingdom, not on earth only, but in heaven.

8. The kingdom of God has been again founded on the earth; the time has come for the Saints to take possession of their own; but by virtue, not by violence — by industry, not by force.

Joseph would appear to have got nearly all these doctrines from Rigdon and Pratt. Pratt — the leading scholar of the Mormon church — too much of a scholar for Young to comprehend and tolerate — has laid down, in various books and lectures, a cosmogony of heaven and earth, which Young has strictly warned us not to receive as truth. Once, if not more than once, Pratt's writings have been formally condemned by the First Presidency and by the Twelve; though he still continues to hold rank as an apostle. "But for me," said Brigham, smiling, "he would have been thrust out of the church long ago." When we put the doctrine of spirit and matter inculcated by Pratt before the President for his opinion, he said, impatiently, "We know nothing about it; it may be all true, it may be all false; we have no light as to those things yet." What has been stated above in the numbered paragraphs is official doctrine taught in the Mormon schools, from the catechism written by Elder Jacques, and formally adopted by Young.

These propositions would seem to have been drawn by the Saints from the oldest and newest mythologies under heaven.

The Mormon God appears to be the same in nature and in shape as Homer's Zeus. Their Angels are not unlike the beni-elohim of St. Paul; not angels and spirits in the old English sense, but rather bodiless and unseen beings, as of fine air and invisible flame. Their Men, as beings which are uncreated, indestructible, are the creations of Pythagoras; and as beings born without sin, accountable only for their own evil deeds, are the fancies of Swedenborg.

Some confusion has arisen, in Utah and elsewhere, as to the Mormon doctrine of angels — a confusion caused by the reveries and speculations of Orson Pratt. Young has been good enough to teach us the true and official belief of his church on this curious subject. Angels, he says, are imperfect beings, incapable of rising into the higher grade of gods, to whom they are now, and will be for ever, the messengers, ministers, and servants. They are immortal beings who have passed through the stage of spirits in space, and of men on earth, but who have not fulfilled the law of life, not spent their strength in perfect obedience to the will of God. Hence they have been arrested in their growth towards the higher state. On my asking in what they had failed to observe the law, Young answered, "In not living the patriarchal life — in not marrying many wives, like Abraham and Jacob, David and Solomon; like all those men who are called in Scripture the friends of God." In fact, according to Young, angels are the souls of bachelors and monogamists; beings incapable of issue, unblessed with female companions, unfitted to reign and rule in the celestial spheres. In the next world, my friend and myself — he being unmarried as yet, and I having only one wife — may only aspire to the rank of bachelor angels, while Young and Kimball are to sit, surrounded by their queens, on celestial thrones!

These notes of the faith, as it is held in Salt Lake City — as it is taught in our own midst — in the Welsh mountains, in the Midland shires, among the Mersey dockmen, in the Whitechapel slums — mystical though they read in the main, exert a mighty spell over the imagination and a mighty power upon the actual life of their people. Nothing is useless in the Mormon system; Nanak himself was not more practical in his reforms than Young. Faith is their principle of action; what they believe they do; and those who would comprehend the position taken up by these Saints on earth — defended by twenty thousand rifles — must try to understand what they think of heaven.

Like the Moslems, the Mormons are a praying people. Religion being their life, every action of the day, whether social or commercial, is considered by them in reference to what may be conceived as the will of God. Hence, they have little respect for policy, caution, compromise; they seem to live without fear; they take no account of the morrow; but trust for safety, succour, and success, to Heaven, and to Heaven alone. Refer, in speaking with them, to the Chicago platform, one of the planks of which is the suppression of polygamy by force, and they only smile at your worldly wisdom, and tell you they are living the divine life, and that God will know how to protect His own. Hint to them that Young is mortal, and will one day need a successor; again they smile at your want of understanding, saying they have nothing to do with such things; that God is wise and strong, capable of raising up servants to guide His church. Their whole dependence seems to be on God. It is right to add — as a point within my knowledge — that they also take good care to keep their powder dry.

Confidence in the divine power to help and save them is not so much the effect of weakness and humility, as of strength and pride. Young puts man much higher in the scale of being than any Christian priest has ever done; higher, perhaps, than any Moslem mollah; though the Koran makes the angels dwelling in Paradise servants of the faithful who are gathered to their rest. Bab in Persia, Nanak in the Punjaub, go beyond Mohammed; teaching their scholars that man is part of the personality of God; but Young describes man as an uncreated, indestructible portion of the Highest; a being with the faculty of raising an order of immortal and unbodied spirits into the exalted rank of gods. How much a high belief in man's rights and powers, as a son of God, and a special favourite of Heaven, can steady the soul in danger, and nerve the arm in battle, was seen in every conflict of the Jews, and is written in every history of the Sikhs.

The secular notes of the Mormon Society may be gathered into three large groups: — (1), Those which define its relations to man as a member and as a stranger; (2), Those which define the method and the principle of its government; (3), Those which define the condition of its family life.

CHAPTER XXV.

Secular Notes.

THE first group of secular notes embraces two leading ideas.

1. The new church, established in Utah, though it is called the Church of America, is free, and (with one passing exception) open to all the world; to men of every race, clime, creed, and colour; taking into its bosom the Jew from New York, the Buddhist from San Francisco, the Parsee from Calcutta, the Wesleyan from Liverpool, the Moslem from Cairo, the Cheyenne from Smoky Hill river.

The one passing exception is the Negro. "The Negro," Brigham said to me this morning, "is a descendant of Cain, the first murderer, and his darkness is a curse put on his skin by God." Only one Negro has ever yet been admitted into brotherhood with the Saints: the act of Joseph, done at Nauvoo. Until God shall have removed this curse, Young will have none of these Cainites in his church.

2. The new church not only receives all comers, but tolerates all dissenters; asking no question, putting no test, demanding no sacrifice. Thus, a man of any other creed may be enrolled among the Saints without losing his identity; without breaking his idols, without rooting up his faith, without shedding his habits; in a word, without that spiritual

change which Christians understand as being born to a new life. The convert to Mormonism accepts a new truth, in addition to the truths which he may have held beforetime. Joseph is proposed to him as a reconciler, not as a separator; the Saints insisting that there is some good in every form of religion, and that no sect on earth enjoys a monopoly in the love of God.

Let us look into these two leading ideas, not in their dogmatical, but in their political aspects.

The church is free and open. — In its first appeals, a new creed has commonly been proposed to a particular race, its ritual adapted to a special zone. We see in history so many examples of such appeals succeeding on the spot, and failing everywhere beyond it, that students are apt to deny the possibility of a common faith, and to treat religion as an affair of climate and of race. The law of Moses made few converts beyond the Hebrew tribes. Confucius finds no followers out of China. The Great Spirit only reigns in the American woods. The Guebres have never carried their worship out of Persia and India. Dagon was a local god, the symbol of a people fond of the sea. Thor is a denizen of the frozen north. Brahma is only known to Hindoos, who make no converts; and so strictly is this law of living apart, for themselves only, fixed in the Hindoo's habits of thought, that a man of one caste can never pass into another; a Brahman born must remain a Brahman; a Sudra born must remain a Sudra all his life. Buddhism has, in some respects, the character of a universal church, having drawn to itself many tribes and nations, and become the chief religion of the world, if the mere number of its temples and congregations could confer that rank; yet among the four hundred millions of men who worship Buddha, there is no instance of a people having ever been converted to the faith in whom the reception of his creed had not been prepared by a natural inclination towards the Oriental belief in transmigration of souls; so that Buddhism itself, however widely it may be diffused throughout the earth, is but the religion of a particular race. Islam is the creed of Arabia and the Arabs. When carried eastward to the Ganges, westward to the Guadalquiver, it was borne forward on the points of a myriad lances, not received by the people of India and of Spain on its merits as a saving faith; and, being neither a natural growth nor a free adoption in those countries, it wore itself out in Spain, while in Persia and India it has rooted itself chiefly among men of Semitic race. Nanak in the Punjab, Bab in Persia, may be said to have founded sects on a wider plan than most other religious leaders: for the Sikhs and Babees are both missionary churches, taking their own from among Moslem, Buddhist, and Hindoo flocks; yet the notion of having one free and open church, which should make the brown man and the white man, the black man and the red man, brothers and equals, has scarcely ever yet dawned upon these fiery advocates of faith.

Thus, nearly all our creeds have either some open or some latent reference to condition. An ancient legend says that the Arabian prophet told his followers they would prevail in arms and plant the true faith wherever the palms bore fruit; a legend which has been almost verified in fact for a thousand years; but Mohammed never dreamt of offering his half-tropical system of social life to the white barbarians of the north; to hungry hunters beyond the Euxine, to frozen woodsmen of the Helvetic Alps. His rule of rejecting wine and pork, wise enough on the Nile and on the Jordan, would have been wasteful of nature on the Danube and the Elbe. His code was written for the palm-bearing zones, and within those zones it has always thriven. No Babee is found settled out of Persia, no Sikh out of Upper India; in each case a man finds his religious rites adapted to the country in which he dwells.

Christianity itself, though nobler in spirit, tougher in framework, than any of these geographical creeds, has yet very much the appearance of being mainly the religion of the Gothic race. Although our creed sprang up in Palestine, and flourished for some years in Egypt and Syria, it never took hold of the Semitic mind, never rooted itself in the Semitic soil. No Arab tribe has been finally won to the Cross, just as no Gothic tribe has been finally gained to the Crescent. The half-Oriental churches which remain in Africa and Asia — the Abyssinian, the Coptic, the Armenian — have no connexion with the great Arabian family of man. In fact, no branch of the Christian society has ever yet clearly put forth the pretension of offering itself to all nations as a free and open church; we pride ourselves on being local and exclusive — Greeks, Latins, Anglicans, Lutherans

— rather than branches of one living, universal church. The largest Christian community on earth defines its Catholicity as Roman and Apostolic, instead of aiming to include the world and owning no founder except Jesus Christ.

How much power is lost by the existence of this parish spirit in our churches, a statesman feels the instant that some object, common to the whole Christian society, comes into view; such as that question of the Holy Sepulchre which, only a dozen years ago, drove the Russ and Frank into fraternal strife.

The new church is tolerant of differences in belief and habits of life. — Laymen like More and Locke have written most eloquently on the policy of tolerating all kinds of opinion; but no large branch of the Christian Church has ever yet entered on the practice of their liberal views. On no better ground than a difference of opinion as to points which only the highest intellects can master, Greek, Roman, Lutheran, Dutch, Genevan, are at deadly feud; mocking each other's rites, impugning each other's motives, condemning each other's actions; saying evil things, doing evil works, to their brethren, with a bitterness of hate increasing with the narrowness of their dividing lines. To wit, the prelates of Rome and England go on damning each other from fast to feast with a ferocity which they would shrink from displaying towards an Imam in Egypt, a Gosain in Bengal, a Prophet at Salt Lake. We make watch-words and warn-words to prevent people from coming near us who might otherwise share in our gospel of love and peace. With as little ruth as the Gileadite swords-mon felt towards the flying bands on the Jordan, we slay all brethren who either can not or will not pronounce our shibboleth.

As our Founder left it, the Church was loving and merciful; as men have made it, it is hard and cruel as a Hindoo caste. A Brahman does not stand aloof from a Sudra with fiercer pride than a Greek Christian shows towards a Copt. Even at the cradle and at the tomb of Christ, we fight for our parish creeds, until the very Bedaween, who have to part the quarrelling disciples, blush for shame. Is it better in London, Rome, and Moscow, than in Bethlehem and Zion? Do the hundred Hindoo sects revile each other in a darker spirit than our own congregations? Who will say it? A worshipper of Vishna may live in the same convent as a worshipper of Siva, and the two Hindoo hermits will dwell in their narrow den in peace. How would it fare in the same shed with a Calvinist and a Catholic? Chaitanya taught the fine truth that faith abolishes and replaces caste; so that Brahman, Kshatrya, Vaisya, and Sudra, whatever their rank and state may be on earth, are equals and brothers in the sight of God. Some Christians preach the same; but where is the national church that has adopted this beneficent truth? Why, a Greek will not allow that a Latin can be saved from hell, and every Armenian monk believes that his Coptic rival will be burnt in everlasting fire. Our churches, even on our parish greens, are worn and torn by internal feuds. Of all races on the earth, the Anglo-Saxon is, in matter of thought and speech, the most liberal, the most tolerant; yet we have had our lurid Smithfield fires, and our list of martyrs lengthens into a mighty host. Within the existing pale we have a High Church faction fighting a Low Church faction, much as Hanafees strive against Malikees in the orthodox Arab mosque. Some writers see a spiritual good in this wide separation of sect from sect; but the political results of it are not to be concealed; and these results are, in England strife, in Europe bloodshed, in Palestine the occupation of our Holy Places by the Turk. A tolerant church would save society from enormous waste of power.

CHAPTER XXVI.

High Politics.

The second group of secular notes — those notes which define the method and the principle of Mormon government — ascend into the highest region of politics. Three points may be mentioned as of supreme importance for the understanding of this peculiar people.

(1.) The new church assumes that God is in personal contact with his Saints; guiding them now, as He did in past times, and as He will do in future times, by a revelation of His will through a chosen seer; not in their great affairs only, their battles, famines, and migrations, but also in their rural and domestic troubles, such as the planting of a field, the building of a store, and the sealing of a wife.

(2.) The new church asserts that true worship is true enjoyment; a blessing from on high, bountifully given by a father to his children; not a tribute levied by a prince, not a penance exacted by a priest; but a light and innocent play, a gladness in the spirit and in the flesh; a sense of duty being done, of service accepted, and of life refreshed.

(3.) In the new church work is honourable, the recovery of barren places noble, the production of corn and oil, of fruit and flowers, of gum and spices, of herbs and trees, a saving act; the whole earth being regarded by the Saints as a waste to be redeemed by labour into the future heaven.

These notes deserve a close attention from those who would comprehend the political growth of the Mormon church.

The new church is divinely ruled. — The notion of God being always present among his people, making known his wishes from day to day, through one selected and unfailing channel, though it may appear to reverential persons very profane, is one that must strike a ruler and thinker, bent on governing men through their hopes and fears, as offering him a vast reserve of strength. Upon a certain class of minds, it is known that the mere sense of distance serves to dim all light, to deaden all fear; so that, with persons having such minds the authority of right and truth is apt to grow faint, in exact proportion to the remoteness of their vouchers. For men of this feeble stamp, everything must be new and near. To them old edicts are of doubtful force; to them ancient traditions are out of date. Indeed, for every one save the highly trained, to whom Euclid is the same as De Morgan, laws have a tendency to become obsolete. A church that takes a particular year as its point of departure, and stands to it for ever, must always reckon on coming into conflict with this weakness of the human heart. To say that a thing is a long way off, that it happened a long time ago, is to express a kind of moral despair. Men wish to get nearer to the sources; if the grace could be given to them, they would like to see God face to face. Moses cannot speak for them; Sinai is but a name.

They never felt the waves of Galilee stilled beneath them. They were not standing in the Gentile court when the Temple vail was rent in twain.

To men of this class, clamorous for a sign, Jerusalem answered by a succession of prophets, who brought the Jewish heaven down to earth, and served it to the people with their daily bread; Rome answers now, as she answered of old, with her mystery of the actual presence of God in the bread and wine. Rome and Jerusalem found in such means a defence against feeble spirits; but cities of a wider culture — London, Boston, Amsterdam, Geneva, — have no resources against such craving of the spirit, excepting the critical opinions of their learned men. But this critical learning does not always answer. A faith which has to find its support in logic and in history, will always appear to some devout and unreasoning minds as a secular sort of canon, resting on man when it should only lean on God. Religious doubt is more exacting, and more illogical, than philosophical doubt. Perhaps the peril arising from its presence in any society is greatest in the freest and most educated states; religious doubt being one of the products of a civilisation quicker in its physical than in its moral growth. As the mind may be clouded with excess of light, it may also become morbid from excess of health. Freedom starts inquiries to which replies are not yet ready, and the philosopher's difficulty makes the impostor's opportunity. When men ask for a sign and receive a date, what marvel if they should turn away? Souls which are groping in the dark do not ask you for controversy, for history, for logic; they want a living gospel, an instant revelation, a personal God.

Here the Saint steps in to supply all wants. When Young, with a peculiar emphasis, says, "This I know," his followers take his voice for that of God. Their eyes dilate, their faces brighten, at his word; new hope, fresh courage, shoot into their hearts. Accepting the counsel, the encouragement, as divine, life begins for them, as it were, anew. It would be simple blindness in our pastors not to see that in our own age, and in the most liberal nations, many weak souls, from lack of true imaginative insight, are falling from a faith which they cannot any longer grasp as they might an actual fact; on one side turning into Rationalism, on the other side into Romanism — here becoming Spiritualists, there inquiring about the Mormons. To the frail who are crying out for guidance, the Reasoners say, Come to us and be cured of creeds; the Saints say, Come to God and be saved from hell.

The service of God is the enjoyment of life. — On its social side, the Mormon church may be regarded as gay, its ritual as festive. All that the elder creeds have nursed in the way of gloom, austerity, bewilderment, despair, is banished from the New Jerusalem. No one fears being damned; no one troubles his soul about fate, free-will, election, and prevenient grace. A Mormon lives in an atmosphere of trust; for in his eyes, heaven lies around him in his glowing lake, in his smiling fields, in his snowy alps. To him, the advent of the Saints was the Second Coming, and the founding of their church a beginning of the reign of God. He feels no dread, he takes no trouble, on account of the future. What is, will be; to-morrow like to-day, the next year like the past one; heaven a continuation of the earth; where to each man will be meted out glory and power according to the fulness of his obedience in the present life. The earth, he says, is a Paradise made for enjoyment. If it were possible to think that Young and Pratt had ever read the Hindoo sages, we should imagine that they had borrowed this part of their system from the disciples of Vallabracha, the prophet of pleasure, the expounder of delight.

From whatever source this idea of a festal service may have come, Euphrosyne reigns in Utah. Young might be described as Minister of Mirth; having built a great theatre, in which his daughters play comedies and interludes; having built a social hall, in which the young of both sexes dance and sing; and having set the example of balls and music-parties both in the open air and under private roofs. Concerts and operas are constantly being given. Water-parties, pic-nics, all the contrivances for innocent amusement, have his hearty sanction. Care is bestowed on the ripening of grapes, on the culture of peaches, on the cooking of food; so that an epicure may chance to find in the New Jerusalem dainties which he would sigh for in vain at Washington and New York. When dining in the houses of apostles, we are always struck with the abundance of sweets and fruits, with the choiceness of their quality, and the daintiness of their preparation. A stranger who sees the Theatre crowded and the Temple unbuilt, might run away with the notion that Young is less of a Saint than his people pretend to think. It would be a mistake; such as we make in Bombay, when we infer that the Maharajahs have no religion because in some of their services they clothe themselves in purple and begin with a feast.

The new church regards work as noble. — That work is noble is a very old phrase, known to the Jews, held by the Essenes, sanctioned by St. Paul. It was a legend among monks in the middle ages; and it lies at the root of all English, French, and American systems for reforming and regenerating society. But the principle that manual labour is good in itself, and for its own sake, a blessing from heaven, a solace to the heart, a privilege, an endowment to the spirit, a service, an act of obedience, has never been taken as her fundamental social truth by any church. Hand-work may have been called useful; it has nowhere been treated by the law as noble. In our old world, the names of prince and gentleman are given to those who write and think, not to those who plough and trench, who throw in the seed and gather up the sheaves. By noble labour, we mean the work of judges, statesmen, orators, priests; no one in Europe would think of saying that to plant a tree, to dig a drain, to build a house, to mow a field, would be noble toil. The Hindoo puts his labourers into the two lowest castes; if they are husbandmen into the third caste, if artisans into the fourth; their estate being in either case far less honourable than that of a warrior, that of a priest. A sudra's soul and body counts for less than one hair from a Brahman's head; for among the Hindoos, work is regarded as a curse, never as a blessing, and the free labourer of Bengal ranks but one degree higher than a pariah and a slave. Now and then the Hebrews had glimpses of a better law: — "Seest thou a man skilful in his work, he shall stand before kings;" the theory of God and Nature; and from this Hebrew source, not from any dreams of Owen, Fourier, and St. Simon, the Saints have borrowed their idea, translating it, not into language only, but into extensive pastures and smiling farms. With them, to do any piece of work is a righteous act; to be a toiling and producing man is to be in a state of grace.

What need is there to dwell on the political value of such a note?

CHAPTER XXVII.

Marriage in Utah.

But the most singular, the most powerful, of these three groups of secular notes, even when we study them from a political point of view only, is that which defines the conditions of family life, particularly in what it has to say of marriage. Marriage lies at the root of society, and the method of dealing with it marks the spirit of every religious system.

Now the new American church puts marriage into the very front of man's duties on earth. Neither man nor woman, says Young, can work out the will of God alone; that is to say, all human beings have a function to discharge on earth — the function of providing tabernacles of the flesh for immortal spirits now waiting to be born — which cannot be discharged except through that union of the sexes implied in marriage. To evade that function is, according to Young, to evade the most sacred of man's obligations. It is to commit sin. An unwedded man is, in Mormon belief, an imperfect creature; like a bird without wings, a body without soul. Nature is dual; to complete his organisation a man must marry a wife. Love, says Young, is the yearning for a higher state of existence; and the passions, properly understood, are the feeders of our spiritual life.

Looking to this dogma of the duty of wedlock

solely as a source of political power, we should have to allow it very great weight. What waste it saves! In many religious bodies marriage is simply tolerated, as the lesser form of two dark evils. Those Essenes from whom we derive so much, allowed it only to the weak, and on account of weakness; they thought it better for a good man to refrain from marriage; and in the higher grades of their society the relation of wife and husband was unknown. Many orders among the Hindoos practise celibacy. The Greeks had their Vestal virgins, the Egyptians their anchorites, the Syrians their ascetics. In the Pagan Olympus, abstinence was a virtue, praised, if not practised, by the gods. Hestia and Artemis were honoured above all the denizens of heaven, because they rose beyond the reach of love; nay, the idea of marriage being a kind of corruption had so far sunk into the pagan mind as to crop out everywhere in the common speech. To be unloved was to be unspotted; to be single was to be pure. In all pagan poetry the title of virgin is held to be higher than that of mother, nobler than that of wife. Among Christian communities marriage is a theme of endless disputation; one church calling it a sacrament, another calling it a contract; all churches considering it optional; few regarding it as meritorious; many denouncing it as a compromise with the devil. The Greek church encourages celibacy in a class; the Latin prohibits marriage to its priests. The Gothic church may be said to stand neutral; but no church in the world has ever yet come to insist on the duty of marriage as necessary to the living of a true Christian life.

On the contrary, every religious body which has dealt with the topic at all — Greek, Armenian, Coptic, Latin, Abyssinian — declares by facts, no less than by words, that any union of the sexes in the bands of wedlock is hostile to the highest conception of a Christian life. Hence the monastic houses; hence the celibacy of priests; institutions which infect the mind of society, arresting the growth of many household virtues, poisoning some of the sources of domestic life. A wifeless priest is a standing protest against wedded love; for if it be true that the human affections are a snare, leading men away from God, it is surely a good man's duty to crush them out. A snare is a snare, a sin a sin, to be avoided equally by the layman and the priest.

Young has turned the face of his church another way. With him marriage is a duty and a privilege; and the elders, being considered examples to the people in all good works, are enjoined to marry. A priest and elder must be a husband; even among the humbler flock, it is held to be a disgrace, the sign of an unregenerated heart, for a young man to be found leading a single life.

But the Saints have pushed the doctrine a step farther; for, instead of denying to their popes and priests the consolation of woman's love, they encourage them to indulge in a plurality of wives; and among their higher clergy — the Prophet, the apostles, and the bishops — this indulgence is next to universal. Not to be a pluralist is not to be a good Mormon. My friend, Captain Hooper, though he is known to be rich, zealous, insinuating — an admirable representative of Utah in Congress — has never been able to rise high in the church, on account of his repugnance to taking another wife. "We look on Hooper," the Apostle Taylor said to me yesterday at dinner, "as only half a Mormon;" at which every one laughed in a sly, peculiar way. When the merriment, in which the young ladies joined, had died down, I said to Hooper, "Here's a great chance for you next season. Pick out six of the prettiest girls in Salt Lake City: marry them in a batch; carry them to Washington; and open your season in December with a ball!" "Well," said Hooper, "I think that would take for a time; but then I am growing to be an old fellow."

Young, who is fond of Hooper, proud of his talents, and conscious of his services, is said to be urging him strongly to marry one more wife at least, so as to cast in his lot finally, whether for good or evil, with the polygamous church. If Hooper yields it will be from a sentiment of duty and fidelity towards his chief.

Every priest of the higher grades in Salt Lake Valley has a plural household; the number of his mates varying with the wealth and character of the elder. No apostle has less than three wives.

Of the marriages of Brigham Young, Heber Kimball, and Daniel Wells, the three members of what is here called the First Presidency, no accounts are kept in the public office. It is the fashion of every pious old lady in this community, who may have lost her husband by death, to implore the bishop of her ward to take measures for getting her sealed to one of these three Presidents. Young is, of course, the favourite of such widows; and it is said that he never makes a journey from the Beehive without being called upon to indulge one of these poor creatures in her wish. Hence, a great many women hold the nominal rank of his wife whom he has scarcely ever seen, and with whom he has never held the relations of a husband, as we in Europe should understand the term.

The actual wives of Brigham Young, the women who live in his houses — in the Beehive, in the Lion House, in the White Cottage — who are the mothers of his children, are twelve, or about twelve, in number. The queen of all is the first wife, Mary Ann Angell, an aged lady, whose five children — three sons, two daughters — are now grown up. She lives in the White Cottage, the first house ever built in Salt Lake Valley. Joseph and Brigham, her eldest sons, chiefs of their race, are already renowned in missionary labours. Sister Alice, her eldest daughter, is my friend — on the stage. The most famous, perhaps, of these ladies is Eliza Snow, the poetess, a lady universally respected for her fine character, universally applauded for her fine talents. About fifty years old, with silver hair, dark eyes, and noble aspect — simple in attire, calm, lady-like, rather cold — Eliza is the exact reverse to any imaginary light of the harem. I am led to believe that she is not a wife to Young in the sense of our canon; she is always called Miss Eliza; in fact, the Mormon rite of sealing a woman to a man implies other relations than our Gentile rite of marriage;

and it is only by a wide perversion of terms that the female Saints who may be sealed to a man are called his wives. Sister Eliza lives in the Lion House, in a pretty room, on the second floor, overlooking the Oquirrh mountains, the Valley, the River Jordan, and the Salt Lake; a poet's prospect, in which form and colour, sky and land and water, melt and fuse into a glory without end. Young's less distinguished partners are: Sister Lucy, by whom he has eight children; Sister Clara, by whom he has three children; Sister Zina, a poetess and teacher (formerly the wife of Dr. Jacobs), by whom he has three children; Sister Amelia, an old servant of Joseph, by whom he has four children; Sister Eliza (2), an English girl (the only Englishwoman in the Prophet's house), by whom he is said to have four or five children; Sister Margaret, by whom he has three or four children; Sister Emiline, often called the favourite, by whom he has eight children. Young himself tells me, that he has never had, and never will have, a favourite in his house; since desires and preferences of the flesh have no part in the family arrangements of the Saints.

The Apostles have fewer blessings than the Presidents; but the Twelve are all pluralists. The following figures are supplied to me by George A. Smith, cousin of the Prophet Joseph, and Historian of the Church, —

> Orson Hyde, first apostle, has four wives;
> Orson Pratt, second apostle, has four wives;
> John Taylor, third apostle, has seven wives;

Wilford Woodruff, fourth apostle, has three wives;
George A. Smith, fifth apostle, has five wives;
Amasa Lyman, sixth apostle, has five wives;
Ezra Benson, seventh apostle, has four wives;
Charles Rich, eighth apostle, has seven wives;
Lorenzo Snow, ninth apostle, has four wives;
Erastus Snow, tenth apostle, has three wives;
Franklin Richards, eleventh apostle, has four wives;
George Q. Cannon, twelfth apostle, has three wives.

With the exception of John Taylor, the apostles are considered poor men; and in Salt Lake it is held dishonest for a man to take a new wife unless he can maintain his family in comfort, as regards lodging, food, and clothes. Some of the rich merchants are encouraged by Young to add wife on wife. A bold and pushing elder said to me last night, in answer to some banter, "I shall certainly marry again soon; the fact is, I-mean to rise in this church; and you have seen enough to know that no man has a chance in our society unless he has a big household. To have any weight here, you must be known as the husband of three women."

CHAPTER XXVIII.

Polygamous Society.

On the political strength which this fashion of plurality lends to the Saints of Salt Lake City, a few words may be said. Two questions present themselves, — In the first place, has the promise of a plurality of wives proved to be a good bribe, inducing men of a certain class to join the Mormon Church? And, in the second place, has the practice of plurality shown itself to be a means by which, when converts have been won, they can be made to multiply in numbers far beyond the ordinary rate?

To the first query, only one answer can be truly given. Name the motive as you please; call it, with the Saints, desire of the spirit; call it, with the Gentiles, desire of the flesh; the fact will remain, — that a license for making love to many women, for sealing them as wives, for gathering them into secluded harems, has acted in the past, and is acting in the present, as a powerful and seductive bribe.

Young and Pratt declare that the carnal appetites have no immediate share in their own selection of brides; that this business of selection is the work of Heaven; that the act of sealing is a religious rite; and that a wife for eternity, the queen and partner of a celestial throne, can be given to a man by none but God. Young told me, with a laughing eye, that they would put their wives in evidence of what they say; many of these ladies being old, plain, uneducated, ill-mannered; though others, as my eyes inform me, are young, fresh, delicate, and charming. But, who can doubt that Young, with his keen sense of power, and his mastery of all the springs of action, is well aware of the political uses to be made of this great appeal of beauty to the carnal man? If taking a fresh wife once a-year be an act of obedience, it serves the Saints very much like a call of pleasure. Yet, who shall say they are insincere? Young told me that in the early days of their strange institution, he was much opposed to plural households, and I am confident that he speaks the truth. Among the Mormon presidents and apostles, we have not seen one face on which liar and hypocrite were written. Though we daily meet with fanatics, we have not seen a single man whom we can call a rogue. Their faith is not our faith, their practice is not our practice. What then? Among the Hindoos, many sects indulge in rites which English people call licentious; some, indeed, being so abominable, that a man who sees them for the first time is apt to call for the police. Could the Ras Mandali be performed in London? Would the Kanchuliyas be allowed to celebrate their worship in New York? Yet there are men and women, living under the sceptre of Victoria, who in perfect faith, if not in perfect innocency, imitate the amorous sports of Krishna, choosing the partners of their delirious worship by the lottery of the vest.

Young may believe in what he says, and in what he does (for I think him, in the sphere of his knowledge, and his customs, an honest man); but some of his followers are accused of taking pains to preach a plurality of wives, as one of the rewards of conversion to his church; and I know that they are fond of quoting the promise made by Nathan to David, that he should wed and enjoy the wives of his enemy Saul. That this gospel of indulgence is found by the Saints to be most alluring in Gentile lands, their missionaries would certainly not deny. It may be that either the flesh is weak or the spirit strong; but the Welsh peasant, he London tailor, the Lancashire weaver, is found to pore with a rapt eye and a burning pulse over the pictures painted by missionaries of that Paradise near Salt Lake, in which a man is free to do all things that his arm can compass, to have as many houses as he can build, as many wives as he can feed and govern. An unregenerate man is told that a harem may be not only lawfully kept, but easily gained — the female heart being opened by a special providence to the truth as it lies in Young — that there are plenty of beautiful girls at Salt Lake; and that a Saint is invited and enjoined to live up to the perfect law. Few elders, it is said, come back to Utah from a journey without bringing a new favourite, won from among the Gentiles to his fold. One of Young's wives was a married lady in New York, who fell in love with the Prophet and fled with him from her husband's house. It is one of the pleasantries of Utah, that Kimball never lets a missionary go forth on a journey without giving him injunctions to bring back young lambs. It is noted, as a rule, that the high dignitaries of the church have been blest by heaven with the prettiest women; one of those recompenses of a virtuous life which Helvetius conceived as desirable, but which no society has ever yet had the wit and daring to adopt.

To the second query two answers may be returned. In a fixed society, like that of Turkey, of Syria, of Egypt, the existence of polygamy would have no great influence on the powers of increase. Once, indeed, men thought otherwise. Writers, like Montesquieu, seeing that polygamy prevailed in many parts of the East, imagined that in these regions the females must be far in excess of the males, and that the appropriation of several women to one man was a rule of nature, made from the earliest times, by way of correcting a freak of birth. Travellers, like Niebuhr, finding his Arab sheikhs with harems, hinted that polygamy arose from the circumstance that Arab women grow old and barren while their husbands are still young and hale. These delusions have long since gone the way of all error.

Now, we can happily say, in the light of science, that even in Egypt and Arabia the males and females are born in about equal numbers; the males being a little in excess of the females. We see, then, that Nature has put the human family on the earth in pairs; rejecting by her own large mandate all those monstrous and irregular growths apart from the conjugal relations established by herself between male and female; whether those growths have taken the shape either of polygamy or of polyandry, either many wives to one husband, or many husbands to one wife. The true law of nature, therefore, is, that one male and one female shall make their home together; and in an old country, where the sexes are equal, where the manners are uniform, and where the religion is common, any departure from this true law will rather weaken than increase the multiplying power of the country as a whole. So far the answer seems to go one way. The question, however, is, not as to the growth of a whole nation: but as to that of a particular family, of a particular community, of a mere sect within the boundaries of that nation. Even in Arabia, it is clear that if a particular sheikh could invent some means of getting from other tribes a great many of their women, until he had enough females in his power to give three wives to every male adult in his camp, the tribe of that sheikh would increase in numbers faster than their neighbours who had only one wife apiece. This is something like the case in America with the Saints. Their own society could not give them the plurality of wives which they announce as the social law of all coming time. But granted that, by either good or evil means, they could get the women into their cnurch, it is idle to deny that the possession of such a treasure gives them enormous powers of increase. One man may be the father of a hundred children; one woman can hardly be the mother of a score. We know that Jair and Hillel must have been polygamists, the moment we hear that the first had thirty sons and the second had forty sons.

It is not an easy thing to count the number of children in the different households at Salt Lake. The census papers cannot be quoted, since they were made up, the Apostle Taylor tells me, mainly by guessing on the part of a Gentile officer, who would not go about and count. In this city, a Moslem jealousy appears to guard such facts as would be public property in London and New York. Young tells us he has forty-eight children now alive. Kimball has, perhaps, an equal number. Every house seems full; wherever we see a woman, she is nursing; and in every house we enter two or three infants in arms are shown to us. This valley is, indeed, the true baby land. For a man to have twenty boys and girls in his house is a common fact. A merchant, with whom we were dining yesterday, could not tell us the number of his children until he had consulted a book then lying on his desk. One of his wives, a nice English lady, with the usual baby at her breast, smiled sweet reproof on his ignorance; but the fact was so; and it was only after counting and consulting that he could give us the exact return of his descendants. This patriarch is thirty-three years old.

It was by means of polygamy that Israel increased in a few generations so as to confound all sense of numbers; and no one can mistake the tendency among these American Saints. Young has more children than Jair; Pratt than Hillel; Kimball than Ibzan. This rate of growth may not be kept up for a hundred years; in time it must slacken of itself for want of supplies; but for the present moment it exists: — not the least ominous of those facts which a statesman of the New America has to face.

CHAPTER XXIX.

The Doctrine of Pluralities.

WHEN the Saints were engaged in seizing, as they say, for their own use, all that was found to be fair and fruitful in other creeds, they would appear to have added to the relations of husband and wife, as these have been fixed by the codes of all civilised states, whether Christian, Moslem, Jewish, or Hindoo, some highly dramatic details. Not only have the Saints adopted polygamy into their church, but they have borrowed it under its oldest and most savage form.

Taken by itself, apart from surrounding schools of thought, the mere fact of a new church having brought itself to allow plurality of wives among its members, would not need to startle us very much, since many of us are familiar with such a system in legend and in history, even though we may be strangers to it by actual sight and sound. Abraham and David practised it. Neither Moses nor Paul forbade it; and Mohammed, while purifying it of the grosser Oriental features, sanctioned it by his words and sanctified it by his deeds. Polygamy enters into the poetry of Cordova, the romance of Bagdad. The enterprising Jain, the learned Brahman, the fiery Rajpoot, all embrace it. Even in the Christian Church, opinions are divided as to whether it is wrong in itself, or only a trouble in the social body.

Many of the early converts, both in Syria and in Egypt, were polygamists; and the questions which have recently disturbed Colenso and the Kaffir chief had arisen in primitive times, when the policy of admitting men having several wives into fellowship was affirmed by fathers of the church. Nor would the appearance of polygamy in these plains of Salt Lake be a novel and surprising fact, since everything that we know of Ute and Shoshonee compels us to believe that plurality has always been the domestic law of these valleys. The sides of these sierras are wild and bare; a poor country and a hard life induce polygamy; and all the tribes of red men which seek a scanty subsistence in these glens and plains practise the nomadic custom of stealing and selling squaws. A big chief prides himself on having plenty of wives; and the white men, who have come to live among these Utes, Cheyennes, Arappahoes, and Kiowas, whether they began as trappers, guides, interpreters, or hunters, have almost always fallen into the Indian way of living. The dozen pale-faces, known to be dwelling with Indian tribes at this moment — hunting buffalo, cutting scalps — are all polygamists; often with larger harems than the biggest native chiefs.

But, the Saints have not simply revived polygamy in Utah; they have returned to that form of domestic life in both its unlimited and its incestuous forms. In their search for the foundations of a new society, they have gone back to the times when Abram was called out of Hauran; undoing the work of all subsequent reformers; setting aside not only

THE DOCTRINE OF PLURALITIES. 253

all that Mohammed, but all that Moses had done for the better regulation of our family life. Moses forbade a man to take a wife of his own flesh and blood. Mohammed restrained his followers to a harem of three or four wives; a moderation at which Young and Kimball, who appeal from Moses to Abraham, only laugh. Who, they ask, married his half-sister Sarai? — the man of God. Hence the Saints of Utah have set up a claim to marry their own half-sisters, without being able to plead for this practice either the Arab custom or the Arab need. They find no objection, either in nature or in revelation, to the custom of breeding in and in; a subject on which we one day had a curious talk with Young and the Twelve. Young denied that degeneracy springs from marriage between men and women who may be near in blood.

The Saints go much beyond Abram; and I, for one, am inclined to think that they have found their type of domestic life in the Indian's wigwam rather than in the Patriarch's tent. Like the Ute, a Mormon may have as many wives as he can feed; like the Mandan, he may marry three or four sisters, an aunt and her niece, a mother and her child. Perhaps it would not be too much to say that in the Mormon code there is no such crime as incest, and that a man is practically free to woo and wed any woman who may take his eye.

We have had a very strange conversation with Young about the Mormon doctrine of incest. I asked him whether it was a common thing among the Saints to marry mother and daughter; and, if so, on what authority they acted, since that kind of union was not sanctioned either by the command to Moses or by the "revelation" to Smith. When he hung back from admitting that such a thing occurred at all, I named a case in one of the city wards, of which we had obtained some private knowledge. Apostle Cannon said that in such cases the first marriage would be only a form; that the elder female would be understood as being a mother to her husband and his younger bride; on which I named my example: one in which an elder of the church had married an English woman, a widow, with a daughter then of twelve; in which the woman had borne four children to this husband; and in which this husband had married her daughter when she came of age.

Young said it was not a common thing at Salt Lake.

"But it does occur?"

"Yes," said Young, "it occurs sometimes."

"On what ground is such a practice justified by the church?"

After a short pause, he said, with a faint and wheedling smile: "This is a part of the question of incest. We have no sure light on it yet. I cannot tell you what the church holds to be the actual truth; I can tell you my own opinion; but you must not publish it — you must not tell it — lest I should be misunderstood and blamed." He then made to us a communication on the nature of incest, as he thinks of this offence and judges it; but what he then said I am not at liberty to print.

As to the facts which came under my own eyes, I am free to speak. Incest, in the sense in which we use the word — marriage within the prohibited degrees — is not regarded as a crime in the Mormon church. It is known that in some of these saintly harems, the female occupants stand to their lords in closer relationship of blood than the American law permits. It is a daily event in Salt Lake City for a man to wed two sisters, a brother's widow, and even a mother and daughter. A saint named Wall has married his half-sister, pleading the example of Sarai and Abraham, which Young, after some consideration, allowed to be a precedent for his flock. In one household in Utah may be seen the spectacle of three women, who stand towards each other in the relation of child, mother, and grand-dam, living in one man's harem as his wives! I asked the President, whether, with his new lights on the virtue of breeding in and in, he saw any objection to the marriage of brother and sister. Speaking for himself, not for the church, he said he saw none at all. What follows I give in the actual words of the speakers: —

D. "Does that sort of marriage ever take place?"

Young. "Never."

D. "Is it prohibited by the church?"

Young. "No, it is prohibited by prejudice."

Kimball. "Public opinion won't allow it."

Young. "I would not do it myself, nor suffer any one else, when I could help it."

D. "'Then you don't prohibit, and you don't practise it.'"

Young. "My prejudices prevent me."

This remnant of an old feeling brought from the Gentile world, and this alone, would seem to prevent the Saints from rushing into the higher forms of incest. How long will these Gentile sentiments remain in force? "You will find here," said Elder Stenhouse to me, talking on another subject, "polygamists of the third generation; when these boys and girls grow up, and marry, you will have in these valleys the true feeling of patriarchal life. The old world is about us yet, and we are always thinking of what people may say in the Scottish hills and the Midland shires."

A revival of polygamy, which would have been singular in either Persia or Afghanistan, sprang up slowly, and by a sort of secret growth. It began with Rigdon and his theory of the spiritual wife, which he is said to have borrowed from the Vermont Methodists. At first, this theory was no more than a mystical speculation; having reference, less to the world and its duties, than to heaven and its thrones. We know that it was preached by Rigdon, that it was denounced by Joseph, that it crept into favour with the elders, that it gave rise to much scandal in the Church, and that it was finally superseded by a more practical and useful creed.

The spirit evoked by that fanatic in the infant church could not be laid; sealing women went on; at first in the new Prophet's household, afterwards in the harems of Kimball, Pratt, and Hyde; whose

THE DOCTRINE OF PLURALITIES.

marriages, only half secret, put an end to the mystical restraints involved in the theory of spiritual husbands and spiritual wives. They were polygamous, but polygamous without disguise. Years afterwards, Young produced a paper, which he said was a true copy of a revelation made to Joseph at Nauvoo, commanding him, after the manner of Abraham, of Jacob, and of David, to receive into his bosom as many wives as should be given unto him of God. This paper was not in Joseph's handwriting, nor in that of Emma, his wife. Young declares that it was written down from the Prophet's lips by a male disciple; adding, with a true touch of nature, that when Emma had first heard it read, she had seized the paper and flung it on the fire.

Young tells me that he was himself opposed to the doctrine, and that he preached against it, foreseeing what trouble it would bring upon the Church. He says that he shed many bitter tears over the sacred writing; and that only on his being convinced by Joseph that the command to marry more wives was a true revelation, he submitted his prejudices and his passions to the will of God. He is very emphatic on this point. "Without this revelation on polygamy," he said to us, "we should have lived our religious life, but not so perfectly as we do now. God directed men, through Joseph, to take more wives. This is what we most firmly believe." As he spoke, he appealed to the apostles who were sitting round us, every one of whom bowed and acquiesced in these words.

For years, the Saints admit that nothing had

come of this revelation; that it was kept a secret from the world; two things having to be seen before such a dogma could be openly proclaimed in the Church: (first) how it would be received by the great masses of the Saints at home and abroad; and (second) how it would be regarded by the American courts of law. To ascertain how it would be welcomed by the Saints, sermons were preached and poetry was composed. Female missionaries called on the people to repent of their sins, and return to the principles of patriarchal life. Every Sarai was encouraged to bring forth her Hagar. A religious glow ran through the Mormon society, and the whole body of Saints declared for publishing the command from God to Joseph in favour of taking to his bosom a plurality of wives.

Two thousand elders came together in the New Jerusalem, and after hearing a discourse from Orson Pratt, and a speech from Brigham Young, they received and adopted the revelation, (August 29, 1852); a remarkable date in the history of their church, one of the saddest epochs in that of the Saxon race.

Nearly all those elders were men of English blood; a few only were Germans, Gauls, and Danes; nineteen in every twenty, at least, were either English or American born. That day the red men and the white men made with each other an unwritten covenant, for the Shoshonee had at length found a brother in the Pale-face, and the Pawnee saw the morals of his wigwam carried into the Saxon's ranch.

But the new dogma from Heaven was announced

by Young as a special and personal, rather than a common and indiscriminate, property of the Saints. The power to take many wives was given to them as a grace, not as a right. Plurality was permitted to a few, not enjoined upon the many. In the eyes of Young, it was regarded, not as a privilege of the earth, but as a gift of heaven; a peculiar blessing from the Father to some of His most favoured sons.

The Prophet seems to have noted from the first, that in this passionate and robust society, full of young life and young ideas, his power of giving women to his elders and apostles would be of higher moment to him, as a governing force, than even his power of blessing the earth and unlocking the gates of heaven. Such an authority has made him the master of every house in Utah. No Pope, no Caliph, no Gosain, ever exercised this power of gratifying every heart that lusted after beauty; but when it came into Young's hands, through the march of ideas and events, he held it in his grip, as a faculty inseparable from his person and his rank. A saint may wed one woman without seeking leave from his Prophet; that privilege may be considered one of his rights as a man; but beyond this limit he can never go, except by permission of his spiritual chief. In every case of taking a second wife, a special warrant is required from Heaven, which Young alone has the right to ask. If Young says yea, the marriage may take place; if he says nay, there is no appeal from his spoken word. In the Mormon church polygamy is not a right of man but a gift of God.

CHAPTER XXX.

The Great Schism.

THIS dogma of a plurality of wives has not come into the Church without fierce disputes and a violent schism.

George A. Smith, cousin of Joseph, and Historian of the Mormon Church, tells me from the papers in his office, that about five hundred bishops and elders live in polygamy in the Salt Lake valleys; these five hundred elders having, as he believes, on the average, about four wives each, and probably fifteen children; so that this very peculiar institution has come, in fourteen years, to affect the lives and fortunes, more or less, of ten thousand persons. This number, large though it seems, is but a twentieth part of the following claimed by Young. Assuming, then, that these five hundred pluralists are all of the same opinion; — in the first place, as to the divine will having been truly manifested to Joseph; in the second place, as to that manifestation having been faithfully recorded; and in the third place, as to that record having been loyally preserved — there must still be room for a very large difference of opinion. The great body of male Saints must always be content with a single wife; Young himself admits so much. Only the rich, the steadfast, the complaisant, can be indulged in the luxury of a harem even now, when the thing is fresh and the number of female converts is large enough to supply the want. As nature itself is fighting against this dogma, the humble Saint cannot hope to enjoy in the future any of the advantages which he is now denied. Many, even among the wealthy, hesitate, like Captain Hooper, to commit themselves for ever to a doubtful rule of family order, and to a certain collision with the United States. Some protest in words, and some recede from the Church, without, however, renouncing the authority of Joseph Smith.

The existence of a second Mormon Church, — of a great schismatic body, is not denied by Young, — who of course considers it the devil's work. Vast bodies of the Saints have left the Church on account of polygamy; twenty thousand, I am told, have done so, in California alone. Many of these non-pluralist Saints exist in Missouri and in Illinois. Even among those who fondly cling to their Church at Salt Lake City, it is apparent to me that nineteen in twenty have no interest, and not much faith, in polygamy. The belief that their founder Joseph never lived in this objectionable state is widely spread.

Prophets, bishops, elders, all the great leaders of the faith, assert that for months before his death at Carthage, the founder of Mormonism had indulged himself, though in secret, with a household of many wives. Of course they do not call his sealing to himself these women an indulgence; they say he took to himself such females only as were given to him of God. But they claim him as a pluralist.

Now, if this assertion could be proved, the trouble would be ended, since anything that Joseph practised would be held a virtue, a necessity, by his flock. On the other side, a pluralist clergy is bound to maintain the truth of this hypothesis. For if Joseph were not a polygamist, he could hardly, they would reason, have been a faithful Mormon and a saint of God; since it is the present belief of their body that a man with only one wife will become a bachelor angel, a mere messenger and servant to the patriarchal gods. So without producing much evidence of the fact, the elders have stoutly asserted that Joseph had secretly taken to himself a multitude of women, three or four of whom they point out to you, as still living at Salt Lake in the family of Brigham Young.

Still, no proof has ever yet been adduced to show that Joseph either lived as a polygamist or dictated the revelation in favour of a plurality of wives. That he did not openly live with more than one woman is admitted by all, — or by nearly all; and so far as his early and undoubted writings are concerned, nothing can be clearer than that his feelings were opposed to the doctrines and practices which have since his death become the high notes of his church. In the Book of Mormon he makes God Himself say that He delights in the chastity of women, and that the harems of David and Solomon are abominations in His sight. Elder Godbe, to whom I pointed out this passage, informed me that the bishops explain away this view of polygamy, as being uttered by God at a time when He was angry with His people, on account of their sins, and as not expressing His permanent will on the subject of a holy life.

The question of fact is open like the question of inference. Joseph, it is well known, set his face against Rigdon's theory of the spiritual wife; and it is equally well known that he neither published the revelations which bear his name, nor spoke of such a document as being in his hands.

Emma, Joseph's wife and secretary, the partner of all his toils, of all his glories, coolly, firmly, permanently denies that her husband ever had any other wife than herself. She declares the story to be false, the revelation a fraud. She denounces polygamy as the invention of Young and Pratt — a work of the devil — brought in by them for the destruction of God's new church. On account of this doctrine, she has separated herself from the Saints of Utah, and has taken up her dwelling with what she calls a remnant of the true church at Nauvoo.

The four sons of Joseph — Joseph, William, Alexander, David — all deny and denounce what they call Young's imposture of plurality. These sons of Joseph are now grown men; and their personal interests are so clearly identified with the success of their father's church, to the members of which their fellowship would be precious, that nothing less than a personal conviction of the truth of what they say can be honestly considered as having turned them against Brigham Young.

As it is, these sons of the original seer have formed a great schism in the church. Under the name of Josephites, a band of Mormons are now gathering round these sons of the Prophet, strong enough to beard the lion in his den. Alexander Smith has been at Salt Lake while I have been here, and has been suffered to preach against polygamy in Independence Hall.

Young appears to me very sore on account of these young men, whom he would gladly receive into his family, and adopt as his sons, if they would only let him. David he regards with a peculiar grace and favour. "Before that child was born," he said to me one day, when the conversation turned on these young men, "Joseph told me that he would be a son; that his name must be David; that he would grow up to be the guide and ruler of this church." I asked Young whether he thought this prophecy would come to pass. "Yea," he answered; "in the Lord's own time, David will be called to this work." I asked him, whether David was not just now considered to be out of the church.

"He will be called and reconciled," said Young, "the moment he feels a desire to be led aright."

This schism on account of polygamy — led, as it is, by the Prophet's widow and her sons — is a serious fact for the church, even in the judgment of those bishops and elders, who in minor affairs would seem to take no heed for the morrow. Young is alive to it; for in reading the Chicago platform, he can see how easily the Gentile world might reconcile itself to the Prophet's sons in Nauvoo, while waging war upon himself and the supporters of polygamy in Utah,

The chief — almost the sole — evidence that we have found in Salt Lake City in favour of Joseph having had several wives in the flesh is an assertion made by Young.

I was pointing out to him the loss of moral force to which his people must be always subject while the testimony on that cardinal point of practice is incomplete. If Joseph were sealed to many women, there must be records, witnesses, of the fact; where are those records and those witnesses?

"I," said Young, vehemently, "am the witness. I myself sealed dozens of women to Joseph."

I asked him whether Emma was aware of it. He said he guessed she was; but he could not say. In answer to another question, he admitted that Joseph had no issue by any of these wives who were sealed to him in dozens.

From two other sources we have obtained particles of evidence confirming Young's assertion. Two witnesses, living far apart, unknown to each other, have told us they were intimate with women who assert that they had been sealed to Joseph at Nauvoo. Young assures me that several old ladies, now living under his roof, are widows of Joseph; and that all the apostles know them, and reverence them as such. Three of these ladies I have seen in the Tabernacle. I have learned that some of these women have borne children to the second Prophet, though they bore none to the first.

My own impression (after testing all the evidence to be gathered from friend and foe) is, that these old ladies, though they may have been sealed to Joseph for eternity, were not his wives in the sense in which Emma, like the rest of women, would use the word wife. I think they were his spiritual queens and companions, chosen after the method of the Wesleyan Perfectionists; with a view, not to pleasures of the flesh, but to the glories of another world. Young may be technically right in the dispute; but the Prophet's sons are, in my opinion, legally and morally in the right. It is my firm conviction, that if the practice of plurality should become a permanent conquest of this American church, the Saints will not owe it to Joseph Smith, but to Brigham Young.

CHAPTER XXXI.

Sealing.

Much confusion comes upon us from the use of this word sealing in the English sense of marriage. Sealing may mean marriage; it may also mean something else. A woman can be sealed to a man without becoming his wife, as we have found in the case of Joseph's supposed widows; also in the instance of Eliza Snow, the poetess, who, in spite of being sealed to Young, is called Miss Snow, and regarded by her people as a spinster. Sealing may mean a great deal more, and it may mean a great deal less than marriage. Consummation, necessary in wedlock, is not necessary in sealing. Marriage is secular; sealing is both secular and celestial.

A strange peculiarity which the Saints have intruded into the finer relations of husband and wife is that of continuity. Their rite of sealing man and woman to each other, may be for either time or for eternity; that is to say, the man may take the woman as his wife either for this world only, as we all do in the Christian church, or for this world during life and the next world after death. The Ute has some inkling of the ideas on which these Saints proceed; since he dreams that in the hunting-grounds beyond the sunset he will be accompanied by his faithful dog and by his favourite squaw. The Mosaic Arab, when the thought of a resurrection dawned upon his mind, peopled his heaven with the men and women whom he had known on earth, and among the rights which he carried forward into the brighter land was that of claiming the society of his mortal wife. The Moslem Arab, though he has learned from a later poetry to adorn his paradise with angelic houris, still fancies that a faithful warrior who prays for such a blessing will be allowed to associate in heaven with the humble partner of his cares on earth. It is only in our higher, holier heaven that these human joys and troubles are unknown, that there is no giving and taking in marriage, that the spirits of the just become as the angels of God.

Upon the actual relations of husband and wife, Ute and Arab theories of reunion after death in the old bonds of wedlock have no effect beyond that of exciting a good and loving woman to strive with a warmer zeal to satisfy the affections of her lord, so as to ensure her place by his side in a celestial wigwam, in a paradisiacal tent. But among the Saints of Salt Lake the notion of a marriage for time being a contract, not only different in duration, but also in nature, from the sealing for eternity, has led to very strange and wholly practical results. A Mormon elder preaches the doctrine that a woman who has been sealed to one husband for time may be sealed to another for eternity. This sealing must be done on earth, and it may be done in the lifetime of her earlier lord. In some degree, it is a gift to the woman of a second choice; for among these Saints the female enjoys nearly the same power of selecting her celestial bridegroom as the male enjoys of selecting his mortal bride.

Of course, the question is always coming forward as to what rights over her person on earth this sealing of a woman's soul for eternity confers. May the celestial rite be performed without the knowledge and consent of the husband for time? Can it be completed without invasion of his conjugal claims? Is it clear that any man would suffer his wife to be sealed to another if he were told of the fact, since an engagement for eternity must be of more solemn nature and more binding force than the minor contract for time? Is it not probable that the intimacies of a man and woman who are linked to each other in the higher bond would be more close and secret than the intimacies of earth?

Some Saints deny that it is a common thing in Utah for a woman to be sealed to one man for earth and another man for heaven. It may not be common; but it occurs in more than one family; it gives occasion for some strife; and the humbler Saint has less protection against abuse of such an order than he would like to enjoy. Young is here the lord of all. If the Prophet says to an elder, "Take her," the woman will be taken, whether for good or evil. Often, I am told, these second and superior nuptials are made in secret, in the recesses of the endowment-house, with the help of two or three confidential chiefs. No notice of them is given; it is doubtful whether any record of them is kept. What man, then, with a pretty wife, can feel sure that her virtue will not be tempted by his elders into forming that strange, indefinite relation for another world with a husband of superior rank in the church? The office of priest, of prophet, of seer, has in every country a peculiar charm for women; what curates are in London, abbés in Paris, mollahs in Cairo, gosains in Benares, these elders and apostles are in Utah; with the added grace of a personal power to advance their female votaries to the highest of celestial thrones. Except the guru of Bombay, no priest on earth has so large a power of acting on every weakness of the female heart as a Mormon bishop at Salt Lake. Who shall assure the humbler Saint that priests possessing so much power in heaven and on earth will never, in these secret sealings for eternity, violate his right, outrage his honour, as a married man?

Another familiarity, not less strange, which the Mormons have introduced into these delicate relations of husband and wife, is that of sealing a living person to the dead.

The marriage for time is an affair of earth, and must be contracted between a living man and a living woman; but the marriage for eternity, being an affair of heaven, may be contracted, say these Saints, with either the living or the dead; provided always that it be a real engagement of the persons, sanctioned by the Prophet, and solemnised in the proper form. In any case it must be a genuine union; a true marriage, in the canonical sense, and according to the written law; not a Platonic rite, an attachment of souls, which would bind the two parties together in a mystical bond only. There comes the rub. How can a woman be united in this carnal conjunction to a man in his grave? By the machinery of substitution, say the Saints.

Substitution! Can there be such a thing in marriage as either one man, or one woman, standing in the place of another? Young has declared it. The Hebrews had a glimmering sense of some such dogma, when they bade the younger brother perform a brother's part; and are not all the Saints one family in the sight of God? Among the Hebrews, this rule of taking a brother's widow to wife was an exception to general laws; and in the Arab legislation of Mohammed, it was put away as a remnant of polyandry, a thing abominable and unclean. No settled people has ever gone back to that rule of a pastoral tribe. But Young, who has no fear of science, deals in audacious originality with this and with every other question of female right. A woman may choose her own bridegroom of the skies, but, like the man who would take a second wife, the woman who desires to marry a dead husband, can do it in no other way than on Young's intercession and by his consent. Say, that a girl of erratic fancy takes into her head the notion that she would like to become one of the heavenly queens of a departed saint; nothing easier, should her freak of imagination jump with the Prophet's humour. Young is her only judge, his yea or nay her measure of right and wrong. By a religious act, he can seal her to the dead man, whom she has chosen to be her own lord and king in heaven; by the same act he can give her a substitute on earth from among his elders and apostles; should her beauty tempt his eye, he may accept for himself the office of proxy for her departed saint.

In the Tabernacle I have been shown two ladies who are sealed to Young by proxy as the wives of Joseph; the Prophet himself tells me there are many more; and of these two I can testify that their relations to him are the same as those of any other mortal wives. They are the mothers of children who bear his name. Two of the young ladies whom we saw on the stage, Sister Zina and Sister Emily, are daughters of women who profess to be Joseph's widows. About the story of all these ladies there is an atmosphere of doubt, of mystery, which we can hardly pierce. Two of them live under Brigham's roof; a third lives in a cottage before his gate; a fourth is said to live with her daughter at Cotton Wood Canyon.

My own impression is, that while some of the old ladies may have been sealed to the Prophet as his spiritual wives only, these younger women elected him to be their lord and king years after his death.

Joseph is the favourite bridegroom of the skies. Perhaps it is in nature, that if women are allowed to choose their spouses, they should select the occupants of thrones; certain it is that many Mormon ladies yearn towards the bosom of Joseph, not poetically, as their Christian sisters speak of lying in the bosom of Abraham, but potentially, as the Hindoo votary of Krishna languishes for her darling god.

Young, it is said, keeps all such converts to himself; the dead Prophet's dignity being so high that none save his successor in the temple is considered worthy to be his substitute in the harem. Beauties whom Joseph never saw in the flesh, who were infants and Gentiles when the riots of Carthage took place, are now sealed to him for eternity and are bearing children in his name.

Except the yearning of Hindoo women towards their darling idol, there is perhaps no madness of the earth so strange as this erotic passion of the female Saints for the dead. A lady of New York was smitten by an uncontrollable desire to become a wife to the murdered Prophet. She made her way to Salt Lake, threw herself at Brigham's feet, and prayed with a genuine fervour to be sealed to him in Joseph's name. Young did not want her; his harem was full; his time was occupied; he put her off with words; he sent her away; but the ardour of her passion was too hot to damp, too strong to stem. She took him by assault, and he at length gave way; after sealing her to Joseph for eternity, he accepted towards her the office of substitute in time, and carried her to his house.

On the other side, the Mormons affect to have such power over spirits as to be able to seal the dead to the living. Elder Stenhouse tells me that he has one dead wife, who was sealed to him, by her own entreaty, after her death. He had known this young lady very well; he describes her as beautiful and charming; she had captivated his fancy; and in due time, had she lived, he might have proposed to make her his wife. While he was absent from Salt Lake City on a mission, she fell sick and died; on her death-bed she expressed an ardent wish to be sealed to him for eternity, that she might share the glories of his celestial throne. Young made no objection to her suit; and on Stenhouse's return from Europe to Salt Lake the rite was performed, in the presence of Brigham and others, his first wife standing proxy for the dead girl, both at the altar and afterwards. He counts the lost beauty as one of his wives; believing that she will reign with him in heaven.

CHAPTER XXXII.

Woman at Salt Lake.

AND what, as regards the woman herself, is the visible issue of this strange experiment in social and family life?

During our fifteen days' residence among the Saints, we have had as many opportunities afforded us for forming a judgment on this question as have ever been given to Gentile travellers. We have seen the President and some of the apostles daily; we have been received into many Mormon houses, and introduced to nearly all the leading Saints; we have dined at their tables; we have chatted with their wives; we have romped and played with their children. The feelings which we have gained as to the effect of Mormon life on the character and position of woman, are the growth of care, of study, and experience; and our friends at Salt Lake, we hope, while they will differ very strongly from our views, will not refuse to credit us with candour and good faith.

If you listen to the elders only, you would fancy that the idea of a plurality of wives excites in the female breast the wildest fanaticism. They tell you that a Mormon preacher, dwelling on the examples of Sarai and of Rachel, finds his most willing listeners on the female benches. They say that a ladies' club was formed at Nauvoo to foster polygamy, and to make it the fashion; that mothers preach it to their daughters; that poetesses praise it. They ask you to believe that the first wife, being head of the harem, takes upon herself to seek out and court the prettiest girls; only too proud and happy when she can bring a new Hagar, a new Bilhah, to her husband's arms.

This male version of the facts is certainly supported by such female writers as Belinda Pratt.

In my opinion, Mormonism is not a religion for woman. I will not say that it degrades her, for the term degradation is open to abuse; but it certainly lowers her, according to our Gentile ideas, in the social scale. In fact, woman is not in society here at all. The long blank walls, the embowered cottages, the empty windows, doorways, and verandahs, all suggest to an English eye something of the jealousy, the seclusion, the subordination of a Moslem harem, rather than the gaiety and freedom of a Christian home. Men rarely see each other at home, still more rarely in the company of their wives. Seclusion seems to be a fashion wherever polygamy is the law. Now, by itself, and apart from all doctrines and moralities, the habit of secluding women from society must tend to dim their sight and dull their hearing; for if conversation quickens men, it still more quickens women; and we can roundly say, after experience in many households at Salt Lake, that these Mormon ladies have lost the practice and the power of taking part, even in such light talk as animates a dinner-table and a drawing-room. We have met with only one exception to this rule; that of a lady who had been upon the stage. In some houses, the wives of our hosts, with babies in their arms, ran about the rooms, fetching in champagne, drawing corks, carrying cake and fruit, lighting matches, iceing water, while the men were lolling in chairs, putting their feet out of window, smoking cigars, and tossing off beakers of wine. (N. B. Abstinence from wine and tobacco is recommended by Young and taught in the Mormon schools; but we found cigars in many houses, and wine in all, except in the hotels!) The ladies, as a rule, are plainly, not to say poorly, dressed; with no bright colours, no gay flounces and furbelows. They are very quiet and subdued in manner, with what appeared to us an unnatural calm; as if all dash, all sportiveness, all life, had been preached out of them. They seldom smiled, except with a wan and wearied look; and though they are all of English race, we have never heard them laugh with the bright merriment of our English girls.

They know very little, and feel an interest in very few things. I assume that they are all great at nursing, and I know that many of them are clever at drying and preserving fruit. But they are habitually shy and reserved, as though they were afraid lest your bold opinion on a sunset, on a watercourse, or a mountain-range, should be considered by their lords as a dangerous intrusion on the sanctities of domestic life. While you are in the house, they are brought into the public room as children are with us; they come in for a moment, curtsey and shake hands; then drop out again, as though they felt themselves in company rather out of place. I have never seen this sort of shyness among grown women, except in a Syrian tent. Anything like the ease and bearing of an English lady is not to be found in Salt Lake, even among the households of the rich. Here, no woman reigns. Here, no woman hints by her manner that she is mistress of her own house. She does not always sit at table; and when she occupies a place beside her lord, it is not at the head, but on one of the lower seats. In fact, her life does not seem to lie in the parlour and the dining-room, so much as in the nursery, the kitchen, the laundry, and the fruit-shed.

The grace, the play, the freedom of a young English lady, are quite unknown to her Mormon sister. Only when the subject of a plurality of wives has been under consideration between host and guest, have I ever seen a Mormon lady's face grow bright, and then it was to look a sentiment, to hint an opinion the reverse of those maintained by Belinda Pratt.

I am convinced that the practice of marrying a plurality of wives is not popular with the female Saints. Besides what I have seen and heard from Mormon wives, themselves living in polygamous families, I have talked, alone and freely, with eight or nine different girls, all of whom have lived at Salt Lake for two or three years. They are undoubted Mormons, who have made many sacrifices for their religion; but after seeing the family life of their fellow-Saints, they have one and all become firmly hostile to polygamy. Two or three of these girls are pretty, and might have been married in a month. They have been courted very much, and one of them has received no less than seven offers. Some of her lovers are old and rich, some young and poor, with their fortunes still to seek. The old fellows have already got their houses full of wives, and she will not fall into the train as either a fifth or a fifteenth spouse; the young men being true Saints, will not promise to confine themselves for ever to their earliest vows, and so she refuses to wed any of them. All these girls prefer to remain single, — to live a life of labour and dependence — as servants, chambermaids, milliners, charwomen, — to a life of comparative ease and leisure in the harem of a Mormon bishop.

It is a common belief, gathered in a great measure from the famous letter on plurality by Belinda Pratt, that the Mormon Sarai is willing to seek out, and eager to bestow, any number of Hagars on her lord. More than one Saint has told me that this is true, as a rule, though he admits there may be exceptions in so far as the Mormon Sarai falls short of her high calling. My experience lies among the exceptions solely. Some wives may be good enough to undertake this office. I have never found one who would own it, even in the presence of her husband, and when the occasion might have been held to warrant a little feminine fibbing. Every lady to whom I have put this question flushed into denial, though with that caged and broken courage which seems to characterise every Mormon wife. "Court a new wife for him!" said one 'lady; "no woman could do that; and no woman would submit to be courted by a woman."

The process of taking either a second or a sixteenth wife is the same in all cases. "I will tell you," said a Mormon elder, "how we do these things in our order. For example, I have two wives living, and one wife dead. I am thinking of taking another, as I can well afford the expense, and a man is not much respected in the church who has less than three wives. Well, I fix my mind on a young lady, and consider within myself whether it is the will of God that I should seek her. If I feel, in my own heart, that it would be right to try, I speak to my bishop, who advises and approves, as he shall see fit; on which I go to the President, who will consider whether I am a good man and a worthy husband, capable of ruling my little household, keeping peace among my wives, bringing up my children in the fear of God; and if I am found worthy, in his sight, of the blessing, I shall obtain permission to go on with the chase. Then I lay the whole matter of my desire, my permission and my choice, before my first wife, as head of my house, and take her counsel as to the young lady's habits, character, and accomplishments. Perhaps I may speak with my second wife; perhaps not; since it is not so much her business as it is that of my first wife; besides which my first wife is older in years, has seen more of life, and is much more of a friend to me than the second. An objection on the first wife's part would have great weight with me; I should not care much for what the second either said or thought. Supposing all to go well, I should next have a talk with the young lady's father; and if he consented to my suit, I should then address the young lady herself."

"But before you take all these pains to get her," I asked, "would you not have tried to be sure of your ground with the lady herself? Would you not have courted her and won her good will before taking all these persons into your trust?"

"No," answered the elder, "I should think that wrong. In our society we are strict. I should have seen the girl, in the theatre, in the tabernacle, in the social hall; I should have talked with her, danced with her, walked about with her, and in these ways ascertained her merits and guessed her inclinations; but I should not have made love to her, in your sense of the word, got up an understanding with her, and entered into a private and personal engagement of the affections. These affairs are not of earth, but of heaven, and with us they must follow the order of God's kingdom and church."

This elder's two wives live in separate houses, and seldom see each other. While we have been at Salt Lake, a child of the second wife has fallen sick; there has been much trouble in the house; and we have heard the first wife, at whose cottage we were dining, say she would go and pay the second wife a visit. The elder would not hear of such a thing; and he was certainly right, as the sickness was supposed to be diphtheria, and she had a brood of little folks playing about her knees. Still the manner of her proposal told us that she was no in the habit of daily intercourse with her sister-wife.

It is an open question in Utah whether it is better for a plural household to be gathered under one roof or not. Young sets the example of unity, so far at least as his actual wives and children are concerned. A few old ladies, who have been sealed to him for heaven, whether in his own name or in that of Joseph, dwell in cottages apart; but the dozen women, who share his couch, who are the mothers of his children, live in one block close together, dine at one table, and join in the family prayers. Taylor, the apostle, keeps his families in separate cottages and orchards; two of his wives only live in his principal house; the rest have tenements of their own. Every man is free to arrange his household as he likes; so long as he avoids contention, and promotes the public peace.

"How will you arrange your visits, when you have won and sealed your new wife?" I asked my friendly and communicative elder; "shall you adopt the Oriental custom of equal justice and attention to the ladies laid down by Moses and by Mohammed?"

"By heaven, sir," he answered, with a flush of scorn, "no man shall tell me what to do, except —— " giving the initials of his name.

"You mean you will do as you like?"

"That's just *it*."

And such, I believe, is the universal habit of thought in this city and in this church. Man is king, and woman has no rights. She has, in fact, no recognised place in creation, other than that of a servant and companion of her lord. Man is master, woman is slave. I cannot wonder that girls who remember their English homes should shrink from marriage in this strange community, even though they have accepted the doctrine of Young, that plurality is the law of heaven and of God. "I believe it's right," said to me a rosy English damsel, who has been three years in Utah, "and I think it is good for those who like it; but it is not good for me, and I will not have it."

"But if Young should command you?"

"He won't!" said the girl with a toss of her golden curls, "and if he were to do so, I would not. A girl can please herself whether she marries or not; and I, for one, will never go into a house where there is another wife."

"Do the wives dislike it?"

"Some don't, most do. They take it for their religion; I can't say any woman likes it. Some women live very comfortably together; not many; most have their tiffs and quarrels, though their husbands may never know of them. No woman likes to see a new wife come into the house."

A Saint would tell you that such a damsel as my rosy friend is only half a Mormon yet; he would probably ask you to reject such evidence as trumpery and temporary; and plead that you can have no fair means of judging such an institution as polygamy, until you are able to study its effects in the fourth and fifth generation!

Meantime, the judgment which we have formed about it from what we have seen and heard may be expressed in a few words. It finds a new place for woman, which is not the place she occupies in the society of England and the United States. It transfers her from the drawing-room to the kitchen, and when it finds her in the nursery it locks her in it. We may call such a change a degradation; the Mormons call it a reformation. We do not say that any of these Mormon ladies have been made worse in their moralities and their spiritualities by the change; probably they have not; but in everything that concerns their grace, order, rank, and representation in society, they are unquestionably lowered, according to our standards. Male Saints declare that in this city women have become more domestic, wifely, motherly, than they are among the Gentiles; and that what they have lost in show, in brilliancy, in accomplishment, they have gained in virtue and in service. To me, the very best women appear to be little more than domestic drudges, never rising into the rank of real friends and companions of their lords. Taylor's daughters waited on us at table; two pretty, elegant, English-looking girls. We should have preferred standing behind their chairs and helping them to dainties of fowl and cake; but the Mormon, like the Moslem, keeps a heavy hand on his female folks. Women at Salt Lake are made to keep their place. A girl must address her father as "Sir," and she would hardly presume to sit down in his presence until she had received his orders.

"Women," said Young to me, "will be more easily saved than men. They have not sense enough to go far wrong. Men have more knowledge and more power; therefore they can go more quickly and more certainly to hell."

The Mormon creed appears to be that woman is not worth damnation.

In the Mormon heaven, men, on account of their sins, may stop short in the stage of angels; but women, whatever their offences, are all to become the wives of gods.

CHAPTER XXXIII.

The Republican Platform.

"WE mean to put that business of the Mormons through," says a New England politician; "we have done a bigger job than that in the South; and we shall now fix up things in Salt Lake City."

"Do you mean by force?" asks an English traveller.

"Well, that is one of our planks. The Republican Platform pledges us to crush those Saints."

This conversation, passing across the hospitable board of a renowned publicist in Philadelphia, draws towards itself from all sides the criticism of a distinguished company of lawyers and politicians; most of them members of Congress; all of them soldiers of the Republican phalanx.

"Do you hold," says the English guest; "you as a writer and thinker, — your party, as the representatives of American thought and might, — that in a country where speech is free and tolerance wide, it would be *right* to employ force against ideas — to throw horse and foot into a dogmatic quarrel — to set about promoting morality with bayonets and bowie-knives?"

"It is one of our planks," says a young member of Congress, "to put down those Mormons, who, besides being infidels, are also Conservatives and Copper-heads."

"Young is certainly a Democrat," adds an Able Editor from Massachusetts, himself a traveller in the Mormon land; "we have no right to burn his block on account of his politics; nor, indeed, on account of his religion; we have no power to meddle with any man's faith; but we have made a law against plurality of wives, and we have the power to make our laws respected everywhere in this Republic."

"By force?"

"By force, if we are driven by disloyal citizens to the use of force."

"You mean, then, that in any case you will use force — passively, if they submit; actively, if they resist?"

"That's our notion," replies our candid host. "The government must crush them. That is our big job; and next year we must put it through."

"You hold it right, then, to combat such an evil as polygamy with shot and shell?"

"We have freed four million negroes with shot and shell," replies a sober Pennsylvanian judge.

"Pardon me, is that a full statement of the case? That you have crushed a movement of secession by means of military force is true; but is it not also true that, five or six years ago, every one acknowledged that slavery was a legal and moral question, which, while peace and order reigned in the slave-states, ought not to be treated otherwise than on legal and moral grounds?"

"Yes, that is so. We had no right over the negroes until their masters went into rebellion. I admit that the declaration of war gave us our only standing."

"In fact, you confess that you had no right over the blacks until you had gained, through the rebellion, a complete authority over the whites who held them in bondage?"

"Certainly so."

"If, then, the planters had been quiet; keeping

to the law as it then stood; never attempting to spread themselves by force, as they tried to do in Kansas; you would have been compelled, by your sense of right, to leave them to time and reason, to the exhaustion of their lands, to the depopulation of their States, to the growth of sound economical knowledge — in short, to the moral forces which excite and sustain all social growths?"

"Perhaps so," answers the Able Editor. "The Saints have not yet given us such a chance. They are very honest, sober, industrious people, who mind their own business mainly, as men will have to do who try to live in yon barren plains. They are useful in their way, too; linking our Atlantic states with the Pacific states; and feeding the mining population of Idaho, Montana, and Nevada. We have no ground of complaint, none that a politician would prefer, against them beyond their plural households; but New England is very sore just now about them; for everybody in this country has got into the habit of calling them the spawn of our New England conventicles, simply because Joseph Smith, Brigham Young, Heber Kimball, all the chief lights of their church, happen to be New England men."

"When New England," adds a representative from Ohio, with a laugh, "goes mad on any point, you will find that she contrives in this Republic to have her way."

"When her way is just and open — sanctioned by moral principle and by human experience — it is well that she should have her way. But will Harvard and Yale support an attack by military power on religious bodies because they have adopted the model of Abraham and David? You have in those western plains and mountains a hundred tribes of red-men who practise polygamy; would you think it right for your missionary society to withdraw from among them the teacher and his Bible, and for General Grant to send out in their stead the soldier and his sword? You have in those western territories a hundred thousand yellow men who also practise polygamy; would you hold it just to sink their ships, to burn their ranches, to drive them from your soil, with sword and fire?"

"Their case is different to that of the Saints," rejoins the Able Editor; "these red-skins and yellow-skins are savages; one race may die out, the other may go back to Asia; but Young and Kimball are our own people, knowing the law and the Gospel; and whatever they may do with the Gospel, they must obey the law."

"Of course, everybody must obey the law; but how? Those Saints, I hear, have no objection to your law when administered by judge and jury, only to your law when administered by colonels and subalterns."

"In other words," says the Pennsylvanian judge, "they have no objection to our law when they are left to carry it out themselves."

"We must put them down," cries the young member of Congress.

"Have you not tried that policy of putting them down twice already? You found them twelve thousand strong at Independence, in Missouri; not liking their tenets (though they had no polygamy amongst them then) you crushed and scattered them into thirty thousand at Nauvoo; where you again took arms against religious passion, slew their Prophet, plundered their city, drove them into the desert, and generally dispersed and destroyed them into one hundred and twenty-seven thousand in Deseret! You know that some such law of growth through persecution has been detected in every land and in every church. It is a proverb. In Salt Lake City, I heard Brigham Young tell his departing missionaries, they were not to suggest the beauty of their mountain home, but to dwell on the idea of persecution, and to call the poor into a persecuted church. Men fly into a persecuted church, like moths into a flame. If you want to make all the western country Mormon, you must send an army of a hundred thousand troops to the Rocky Mountains."

"But we can hardly leave these pluralists alone?"

"Why not — so far at least as regards bayonets and bowie-knives? Have you no faith in the power of truth? Have you no confidence in being right? Nay, are you sure that you have nothing to learn from them? Have not the men who thrive where nobody else can live, given ample evidence that, even though their doctrines may be strange and their morals false, the principles on which they till the soil and raise their crops, are singularly sound?"

"I admit," says the Able Editor, "they are good farmers."

"Good is a poor term, by which to express the marvel they have wrought. In Illinois, they changed a swamp into a garden. In Utah, they have made the desert green with pastures and tawny with maize and corn. Of what is Brigham Young most proud? Of his harem, his temple, his theatre, his office, his wealth? He may pride himself on these things in their measure; but the fact of his life which he dwelt upon most, and with the noblest enthusiasm, is the raising of a crop of ninety-three and a half bushels of wheat from one single acre of land. The Saints have grown rich with a celerity that seems magical, even in the United States. Beginning life at the lowest stage, recruited only from among the poor, spoiled of their goods and driven from their farms, compelled to expend millions of dollars in a perilous exodus, and finally located on a soil from which the red-skin and the bison had all but retired in despair, they have yet contrived to exist, to extend their operations, to increase their stores. The hills and valleys round Salt Lake are everywhere smiling with wheat and rye. A city has been built; great roads have been made; mills have been erected; canals have been dug; forests have been felled. A dépôt has been formed in the wilderness from which the miners of Montana and Nevada can be fed. A chain of communication from St. Louis to San Francisco has been laid. Are the Republican majority prepared to undo the progress of twenty years in order to curb an obnoxious doctrine? Are they sure that the attempt being made, it would succeed? What facts in the past history of these Saints permit you to infer that persecution, however sharp, would diminish their number, their audacity, and their zeal?"

"Then you see no way of crushing them?"

"Crushing them! No, none. I see no way of

dealing with any moral and religious question except by moral means employed in a religious spirit. Why not put your trust in truth, in logic, in history? Why not open good roads to Salt Lake? Why not encourage railway communication; and bring the practical intellect and noble feeling of New England to bear upon the household of many wives? Why not meet their sermons by sermons; try their science by science; encounter their books with books? Have you no missionaries equal to Elder Stenhouse and Elder Dewey? You must expect that while you act on the Saints, the Saints will re-act upon you. It will be for you a trial of strength; but the weapons will be legitimate and the conclusions will be blessed. Can you not trust the right side and the just cause, to come out victoriously from such a struggle?"

"Well," says the judge, "while we are divided in opinion, perhaps, as to the use of physical force, we are all in favour of moral force. Massachusetts is our providence; but, after all, we must have one law in this Republic. Union is our motto, equality our creed. Boston and Salt Lake City must be got to shake hands, as Boston and Charleston have already done. If you can persuade Brigham to lie down with Bowles, I am willing to see it.... And now pass the wine."

END OF VOL. I.

PRINTING OFFICE OF THE PUBLISHER.

MRS. GASKELL: Mary Barton 2v. Ruth 2v. North & South 1v. Lizzie Leigh 1v. Charlotte Brontë 2v. Lois the Witch 1v. Sylvia's Lovers 2v. A Dark Night's Work 1v. Wives & Daughters 3v. Cranford 1v. Cousin Phillis 1v.

MRS. GORE: Castles in the Air 1v. The Dean's Daughter 2v. Progress and Prejudice 2v. Mammon 2v. A Life's Lessons 2v. The two Aristocracies 2v. Heckington 2v.

"JOHN HALIFAX," AUTHOR OF: John Halifax 2v. The Head of the Family 2v. A Life for a Life 2v. A Woman's Thoughts about Women 1v. Agatha's Husband 1v. Romantic Tales 1v. Domestic Stories 1v. Mistress and Maid 1v. The Ogilvies 1v. Lord Erlistoun 1v. Christian's Mistake 1v. Bread upon the Waters 1v. A Noble Life 1v. Olive 2v. Two Marriages 1v. Studies from Life 1v. Poems 1v. The Woman's Kingdom 2v. The Unkind Word 2v. A Brave Lady 2v.

MRS. HALL: Can Wrong be Right? 1v.

SIR H. HAVELOCK, by the Rev. Brock, 1v.

HAWTHORNE: The Scarlet Letter 1v. Transformation 2v.

HEMANS: The Select Poetical Works 1v.

HOUSEHOLD WORDS conducted by Ch. Dickens. 1851-1856. 36v. NOVELS and TALES reprinted from Household Words. 11v. 1856-59.

WASH. IRVING: The Sketch Book (portr.) 1v. The Life of Mahomet 1v. Successors of Mahomet 1v. Oliver Goldsmith 1v. Wolfert's Roost 1v. The Life of Washington 5v.

G. P. R. JAMES: Morley Ernstein (w. portr.) 1v. Forest Days 1v. The False Heir 1v. Arabella Stuart 1v. Rose d'Albret 1v. Arrah Neil 1v. Agincourt 1v. The Smuggler 1v. The Stepmother 2v. Beauchamp 1v. Heidelberg 1v. The Gipsy 1v. Ehrenstein 1v. Darnley 1v. Russell 2v. The Convict 2v. Sir Theodore Broughton 2v.

MRS. JENKIN: Who Breaks — Pays 1v. Skirmishing 1v. Once and Again 2v. Two French Marriages 2v. Within an Ace 1v.

DOUGLAS JERROLD: Saint Giles and Saint James 2v. Men of Character 2v.

JOHNSON: Lives of the Poets 2v.

MISS KAVANAGH: Nathalie 2v. Daisy Burns 2v. Grace Lee 2v. Rachel Gray 1v. Adèle 3v. Two Sicilies 2v. Seven Years 2v. French Women of Letters 1v. English Women of Letters 1v. Queen Mab 2v. Beatrice 2v. Sybil's Second Love 2v. Dora 2v.

KIMBALL: St. Leger 1v. Student Life 1v. Undercurrents 1v. Was he Successful? 1v.

KINGLAKE: Eothen 1v. The Invasion of

LEMON: Wait for the End 3v. Loved at Last 2v. Falkner Lyle 2v. Leyton Hall 2v. Golden Fetters 2v.

CHARLES LEVER: The O'Donoghue 1v. The Knight of Gwynne 3v. Arthur O'Leary 2v. Harry Lorrequer 2v. Charles O'Malley 3v. Tom Burke 3v. Jack Hinton 2v. The Daltons 4v. The Dodd Family 3v. The Martins of Cro' Martin 3v. Glencore 2v. Roland Cashel 3v. Davenport Dunn 3v. Con Cregan 2v. One of Them 2v. Maurice Tiernay 2v. Sir Jasper Carew 2v. Barrington 2v. A Day's Ride 2v. Luttrell of Arran 2v. Tony Butler 2v. Sir Brook Fossbrooke 2v. The Bramleighs 2v. A Rent in a Cloud 1v. That Boy of Norcott's 1v.

G. H. LEWES: Ranthorpe 1v. The Physiology of Common Life 2v.

"GUY LIVINGSTONE," AUTHOR OF: Guy Livingstone 1v. Sword and Gown 1v. Barren Honour 1v. Border & Bastille 1v. Maurice Dering 1v. Sans Merci 2v. Breaking a Butterfly 2v.

LONGFELLOW: Poet. Works (portr.) 3v. The Divine Comedy of Dante Alighieri 3v. The New-England Tragedies 1v.

LUTFULLAH, by Eastwick, 1v.

LORD MACAULAY: History of England (w. portr.) 10v. Critical & Historical Essays 5v. Lays of ancient Rome 1v. Speeches 2v. Biographical Essays 1v. William Pitt; Atterbury 1v.

MAC DONALD: Alec Forbes of Howglen 2v. Annals of a Quiet Neighbourhood 2v.

MACLEOD: The Old Lieutenant 1v.

LORD MAHON: vide STANHOPE.

MANSFIELD: The Water Lily 1v.

CAPT. MARRYAT: Jacob Faithful (portr.) 1v. Percival Keene 1v. Peter Simple 1v. Japhet 1v. Monsieur Violet 1v. The Settlers 1v. The Mission 1v. The Privateer's-Man 1v. The Children of the New-Forest 1v. Valerie 1v. Mr. Midshipman Easy 1v. The King's Own 1v.

FLORENCE MARRYAT: Love's Conflict 2v. For Ever & Ever 2v. The Confessions of Gerald Estcourt 2v. Nelly Brooke 2v. Véronique 2v.

MRS. MARSH: Ravenscliffe 3v. Emilia Wyndham 2v. Castle Avon 2v. Aubrey 2v. The Heiress of Haughton 2v. Evelyn Marston 2v. The Rose of Ashurst 2v.

MELVILLE: Kate Coventry 1v. Holmby House 3v. Digby Grand 1v. Good for Nothing 2v. The Queen's Maries 2v. The Gladiators 2v. The Brookes of Bridlemere 2v. Cerise 2v. The Interpreter 2v. The White Rose 2v. M. or N. 1v.

MEREDITH (HON. R. LYTTON): Poems 2v.

MILTON: Poetical Works 1v.

THOMAS MOORE: Poetical Works 5v.

MRS. OLIPHANT: M. Maitland 1 v. Mortimers 2 v. Agnes 2 v. Madonna Mary 2 v. The Minister's Wife 2 v. The Rector etc. 1 v. Salem Chapel 2 v.
OUIDA: Idalia 2 v.
PEARD: One Year 2 v.
TH. PERCY: Reliques of English Poetry 3v.
POPE: Poetical Works (w. portr.) 1 v.
THE PRINCE CONSORT'S Speeches 1 v.
CHARLES READE: "It is never too late to mend" 2 v. "Love me little, love me long" 1 v. The Cloister and the Hoarth 2 v. Hard Cash 3 v.
"RECOMMENDED TO MERCY," AUTHOR OF: Recommended to Mercy 2 v. Zoe's 'Brand' 2 v.
RICHARDSON: Clarissa Harlowe 4 v.
REV. F. W. ROBERTSON: Sermons 4 v.
ROSS: The Pretty Widow 1 v. A London Romance 2 v.
RUFFINI: Lavinia 2 v. Doctor Antonio 1 v. Lorenzo Benoni 1 v. Vincenzo 2 v. A Quiet Nook 1 v. The Paragreens 1 v.
ESTELLE RUSSELL 2 v.
G. A. SALA: The Seven Sons of Mammon 2 v.
"SCHÖNBERG-COTTA FAMILY," AUTHOR OF: Schönberg-Cotta Family 2 v. The Draytons 2 v. On Both Sides of the Sea 2 v. Winifred Bertram 1 v. Diary of Mrs. Kitty Trevylyan 1 v.
W. SCOTT: Waverley (portr.) 1 v. The Antiquary 1 v. Ivanhoe 1 v. Kenilworth 1 v. Quentin Durward 1 v. Old Mortality 1 v. Guy Mannering 1 v. Rob Roy 1 v. The Pirate 1 v. Nigel 1 v. Black Dwarf 1 v. Montrose 1 v. The Bride of Lammermoor 1 v. The Heart of Mid-Lothian 2 v. The Monastery 1 v. The Abbot 1 v. Peveril 2 v. Poetical Works 2 v.
MISS SEWELL: Amy Herbert 2 v. Ursula 2 v. A Glimpse of the World 2 v. The Journal of a Home Life 2 v. After Life 2 v.
SHAKESPEARE: The Plays and Poems (w. portr.) compl. 7 v. — Each Play also at 1/10 Thlr.
SHAKESPEARE: Doubtful Plays 1 v.
SHERIDAN: Dramatic Works 1 v.
SMOLLETT: Roderick Random 1 v. Humphry Clinker 1 v. Peregrine Pickle 2 v.
STANHOPE: History of England 7 v. The Reign of Queen Anne 2 v.
STERNE: Tristram Shandy 1 v. A Sentimental Journey (w. portr.) 1 v.
"STILL WATERS," AUTHOR OF: Still Waters 1 v. Dorothy 1 v. De Cressy 1 v. Uncle Ralph 1 v. MaidenSisters 1 v. Martha Brown 1 v.
MRS. STOWE: Uncle Tom (w. portr.) 2 v. A Key to Uncle Tom 2 v. Dred 2 v. The Minister's Wooing 1 v. Oldtown Folks 2 v.
SUNBEAM STORIES 1 v.
SWIFT: Gulliver's Travels 1 v.
BARONESS TAUTPHOEUS: Cyrilla 2 v. The Initials 2 v. Quits 2 v. At Odds 2 v.
COLONEL MEADOWS TAYLOR: Tara 3 v.
TEMPLETON: Diary and Notes 1 v.
TENNYSON: Poetical Works 6 v.
THACKERAY: Vanity Fair 3 v. Pendennis 3 v. Miscellanies 8 v. Henry Esmond 2 v. The English Humourists 1 v. The Newcomes 4 v. The Virginians 4 v. The Four Georges; Lovel the Widower 1 v. Philip 2 v. Denis Duval 1 v. Roundabout Papers 2 v. Catherine 1 v.

THE NEW TESTAMENT (Vol. 1000.)
THOMAS: Denis Donne 2 v. On Guard 2 v. Walter Goring 2 v. Played Out 2 v. Called to Account 2 v. Only Herself 2 v.
THOMSON: The Seasons (w. portr.) 1 v.
TRAFFORD (MRS. RIDDELL): George Goith of Fen Court 2 v. Maxwell Drewitt 2 v. Race for Wealth 2 v. Far above Rubies 2 v.
TROLLOPE: Doctor Thorne 2 v. The Bertrams 2 v. The Warden 1 v. Barchester Towers 2 v. Castle Richmond 2 v. The West Indies 1 v. Framley Parsonage 2 v. North America 3 v. Orley Farm 3 v. Rachel Ray 2 v. The Small House at Allington 3 v. Can you forgive her? 3 v. The Belton Estate 2 v. The Last Chronicle of Barset 3 v. The Claverings 2 v. Phineas Finn 3 v. He knew he was Right 3 v.
T. A. TROLLOPE: The Garstangs 2 v.
WARBURTON: The Crescent and the Cross 2 v. Darien 2 v.
WARREN: Diary of a late Physician 2 v. Ten Thousand a-Year 3 v. Now and Then 1 v. The Lily and the Bee 1 v.
THE WATERDALE NEIGHBOURS 2 v.
WETHERELL: The wide, wide World 1 v. Queechy 2 v. The Hills of the Shatemuc 2 v. Say and Seal 2 v. The Old Helmet 2 v.
A WHIM and its Consequences 1 v.
MRS. HENRY WOOD: East Lynne 3 v. The Channings 2 v. Mrs. Halliburton's Troubles 2 v. Verner's Pride 3 v. The Shadow of Ashlydyat 3 v. Trevlyn Hold 2 v. Lord Oakburn's Daughters 2 v. Oswald Cray 2 v. Mildred Arkell 2 v. St. Martin's Eve 2 v. Elster's Folly 2 v. Lady Adelaide's Oath 2 v. Orville College 1 v. A Life's Secret 1 v. The Red Court Farm 2 v. Anne Hereford 2 v. Roland Yorke 2 v. George Canterbury's Will 2 v.
WORDSWORTH: Select Poet. Works 2 v.
WRAXALL: Wild Oats 1 v.
EDM. YATES: Land at Last 2 v. Broken to Harness 2 v. Forlorn Hope 2 v. Black Sheep 2 v. The Rock Ahead 2 v. Wrecked in Port 2 v.
MISS YONGE: The Heir of Redclyffe 2 v. Heartsease 2 v. Daisy Chain 2 v. Dynevor Terrace 2 v. Hopes and Fears 2 v. Stepmother 2 v. The Trial 2 v. The Clever Woman 2 v. The Dove in the Eagle's Nest 2 v. The Danvers Papers; the Prince and the Page 1 v. The Chaplet of Pearls 2 v. The Two Guardians 1 v. The Caged Lion 2 v.

DICTIONARY OF THE ENGLISH & GERMAN languages. By James. 20th Ster. Ed. 8°. 1½ ℳ.
DICTIONARY OF THE ENGLISH & FRENCH languages. By James & Molé. 10th St. Ed. 8°. 2 ℳ.
DICTIONARY OF THE ENGLISH & ITALIAN languages. By James & Grassi. 6th Ed 8°. 1¾ ℳ.
NEW POCKET DICTIONARY of the English and German languages. By Wessely. Third Ster. Edition. 16°. ½ ℳ. bound ¾ ℳ.
NEW POCKET DICTIONARY of the English and French languages. By Wessely. Second Ster. Edition. 16°. ½ ℳ. bound ¾ ℳ.
NEW POCKET DICTIONARY of the English and Italian languages. By Wessely. Stereotype Edition. ½ ℳ. bound ¾ ℳ.